FRED ASTAIRE

FRED ASTAIRE

His Friends Talk

Sarah Giles

DOUBLEDAY

New York London Toronto Sydney Auckland

Overleaf: **Under a painting of his favorite horse, Triplicate, at his ranch, Chatsworth, 1952.**

Design by Angle [○] New York

Excerpt from lyrics of "TOP HAT, WHITE TIE AND TAILS" by Irving Berlin on opening page:

© Copyright 1935 Irving Berlin
© Copyright renewed 1962 Irving Berlin
Reprinted by special permission of Irving Berlin Music Corporation.

Published by Doubleday, a division of Bantam Doubleday Dell Publishing Group, Inc.
666 Fifth Avenue, New York, New York 10103
Doubleday and the portrayal of an anchor with a dolphin are trademarks of Doubleday, a division of Bantam Doubleday Dell Publishing Group, Inc.

Library of Congress Cataloging-in-Publication Data
Giles, Sarah.
    Fred Astaire: his friends talk / by Sarah Giles.—1st ed.
        p.   cm.
    1. Astaire, Fred.   2. Dancers—United States—Biography.
3. Actors—United States—Biography.   I. Title.
GV1785.A83G55 1988
793.3'2'0924—dc19
[B]   88-16156
                                                              CIP

ISBN 0-385-24741-9
Copyright © 1988 by Sarah Giles

To my mother and father

WHO'S WHO

Tina Sinatra: friend
Anne Slater: friend
Emma Soames: editor in chief of *Tatler* magazine
Sir Robert Throckmorton: friend
Whitney Tower: friend
Jeremy Tree: friend
Twiggy: friend
Alfred Vanderbilt: friend
Jeanne Vanderbilt: friend
E. P. Varjian: owner of the Premier Market
Diana Vreeland: friend
Robert Wagner: friend
Mrs. Jock Whitney: friend
Bill Winfrey: trainer
Princess Alexandra: friend
Ava Astaire: daughter
David Bailey: photographer
Mikhail Baryshnikov: ballet dancer
Irving Berlin: friend, songwriter
Michael Black: agent
Leslie Caron: friend, dance partner
Caspar of the Bistro: maître d'
Cyd Charisse: friend, dance partner
George Christy: Hollywood columnist
Jo Cody: housekeeper for eight years
Betty Comden: screenwriter
Rocky Converse: friend, Gary Cooper's widow
Don Cook: friend
Mrs. Sammy Davis, Jr.: friend
The Duke of Devonshire: friend
Stanley Donen: friend, director
Peter Duchin: friend, bandleader
Dominick Dunne: friend
Ahmet Ertegun: founder and head of Atlantic Records
Douglas Fairbanks, Jr.: friend
Leonard Gershe: friend, screenwriter
Sam Goldwyn, Jr.: friend
Martha Graham: choreographer
Lily Guest: friend
Jerry Hall: model
Radie Harris: Hollywood columnist

Jack Haley, Jr.: producer
Audrey Hepburn: friend, dance partner
Katharine Hepburn: colleague
Henry Herbert, the Earl of Pembroke: producer
Lester Holt: trainer
Mrs. Lester Holt: friend, wife of trainer
Jean Howard: friend
Michael Jackson: friend
Dani Janssen: actor David Janssen's widow
Molly Keane: friend of Adele's from Ireland, novelist M. J. Farrell
Slim Keith: friend, once married to agent Leland Hayward
Jimmy Kilroe: friend, director of the Santa Anita racetrack
Howard W. Koch: producer
Eleanor Lambert: friend
Irving "Swifty" Lazar: agent
Jack Lemmon: friend
Mrs. Oscar Levant: friend
Carol Lynley: friend
Bob Mackie: clothes designer
Roddy McDowall: friend
Richard McKenzie: son-in-law
Aileen Mehle (Suzy): columnist
Lady Alexandra Metcalfe: friend
Liza Minnelli: friend
David Niven, Jr.: friend
Jamie Niven: friend
Rudolf Nureyev: ballet dancer
Hermes Pan: friend, choreographer
Anthony Perkins: friend
Patricia Prior: friend, companion to Adele
Queen Elizabeth, the Queen Mother: friend
The Rajmata of Jaipur: friend
Gene Rayburn: game show star
Nancy Reagan: friend
Dr. Harry Reizner: podiatrist
Ginger Rogers: dance partner
Herb Ross: director
Bill Self: friend
Mrs. Bill Self: friend
Frank Sinatra: friend

CONTENTS

Returning from Great Britain aboard the S.S. Berengaria, 1931.

Tina Brown, the editor in chief of *Vanity Fair*, soon after Fred Astaire's death, in June 1987, asked me to prepare a tribute to the great artist in the words of those who knew him and loved him best. I interviewed twenty of the people closest to him, traveling over 10,000 miles in Europe and in America. After the article appeared, Jacqueline Onassis telephoned from Doubleday and asked me to expand the material into a book. That led me to sixty-one more of Mr. Astaire's friends and peers.

My foremost thanks, therefore, go to Tina Brown. I am also eternally grateful to the people who, out of their love and admiration for Mr. Astaire, gave me their thoughts, recollections, private photographs, and memorabilia: Her Royal Highness the Princess Alexandria, Ava Astaire McKenzie, David Bailey, Mikhail Baryshnikov, Irving Berlin, Michael Black, Leslie Caron, Casper of the Bistro, Cyd Charisse, George Christy, Jo Cody, Betty Comden, Rocky Converse, Donald Cook, Altovise Davis, the Duke of Devonshire, Stanley Donen, Peter Duchin, Dominick Dunne, Ahmet Ertegun, Douglas Fairbanks Jr., Leonard Gershe, Sam Goldwyn Jr., Martha Graham, Lily Guest, Jerry Hall, Radie Harris, Jack Haley Jr., Audrey Hepburn, Katharine Hepburn, Henry Herbert, Lester Holt, Mrs. Lester Holt, Jean Howard, Michael Jackson, Her Highness the Rajmata of Jaipur, Dani Janssen, Molly Keane, Slim Keith, Jimmy Kilroe, Howard W. Koch, Eleanor Lambert, Swifty Lazar, Jack Lemmon, Mrs. Oscar Levant, Carol Lynley, Bob Mackie, Roddy McDowall, Richard McKenzie, Aileen Mehle, Lady Alexandra Metcalfe, Liza Minnelli, David Niven Jr., Jamie Niven, Rudolf Nureyev, Hermes Pan, Anthony Perkins, Patricia Prior, Her Majesty the Queen Mother, Gene Rayburn, Nancy Reagan, Dr. Harry Reizner, Ginger Rogers, Herb Ross, Bill Self, Peggy Self, Frank Sinatra, Tina Sinatra, Anne Slater, Emma Soames, Sir Robert Throckmorton, Whitney Tower, Jeremy Tree, Twiggy, Alfred Vanderbilt, Jeanne Vanderbilt, E. P. Varjian, Diana Vreeland, Robert Wagner, Mrs. John Hay Whitney, Bill Winfrey.

Since many of these people were unknown to me, I am also indebted to those who brought me in touch with them: John Bowes Lyon, Lady Kitty Giles, Judy Green, Reinaldo Herrera, Fred Hughes, Gita and Sonny Mehta, June Ogilvy, Lisa Robinson, Steve Rubell, Christopher Sykes, Robert Tracy, and Jerome Zipkin.

A special thank-you goes to Morton Janklow, who represented me for this my first book; to Derek Ungless, who designed it; and to Nancy Evans, Jacqueline Onassis, and Judy Sandman at Doubleday.

Last but not least, I am deeply indebted to Wayne Lawson for his expertise and attentiveness at every step in the preparation of the manuscript.

Sarah Giles, New York, July 1988

Fred and Adele in *The Band Wagon*, at the New Amsterdam Theatre, New York, 1931.

Atlantic City, 1920. Adele, Ann, and Fred Astaire.

I'm steppin' out, my dear,
to breathe an atmosphere
that simply reeks with class.
—Irving Berlin

THE ARTIST

THE DANCER

Rehearsing *Top Hat*, 1935.

Fred and Adele Astaire.

Fred Astaire was probably the greatest, most original dancer of all time. George Balanchine and Mikhail Baryshnikov, for two, said so. And because Fred lived in the age of film, he is also the best recorded. He started dancing in vaudeville with his sister, Adele, in 1905. Between 1912 and 1933, they starred in twelve musicals together in America and England. In 1933 Fred went on alone to Hollywood, and between then and 1976 he made thirty-three musical films and partnered a staggering list of Hollywood dancers: Joan Crawford, Dolores Del Rio, Eleanor Powell, Rita Hayworth, Lucille Bremer, Virginia Dale, Paulette Goddard, Joan Leslie, Judy Garland, Ann Miller, Debbie Reynolds, Jane Powell, Betty Hutton, Cyd Charisse, Leslie Caron, Audrey Hepburn, and the remarkable Ginger Rogers, with whom he made ten of his greatest films. Among his male costars were many of the biggest names in Hollywood musicals—Bing Crosby, Oscar Levant, George Murphy, Red Skelton, Gene Kelly, and Tommy Steele. Between 1958 and 1972 he made a series of award-winning television specials in which he introduced the favorite dancing partner of his later years, Barrie Chase. With the completion of his final achievement on film, MGM's two-part That's Entertainment, in 1974 and 1976, he had been a musical star for seventy-one years.

He never worried about his facial expressions until he had his steps.

Leslie Caron

He never stopped dancing. It is a habit in rehearsal halls that when you take a break the pianist goes on doodling. But Fred would start playing with a chair, or with a cane, or a coat that was there—*he* would doodle. I remember going out for air, and as I came back into the rehearsal room, he was dancing a number with a coat hanger.

Stanley Donen

Fred once told me he had a copy of all the musical numbers he'd ever done on film, and I said I would give anything to see them, so he got them out of his basement and I took them to a projection room at MGM. He'd cut out all the singing from every number; all that was there was the dancing. It took me three or four days to look at them.

Diana Vreeland

I went to Harlem one evening in the twenties with Fred and his sister, Adele. Fred was going to have a lesson from Bill "Bojangles" Robinson, whom he admired tremendously. Bojangles taught Fred a shuffle: six steps up and six steps down. That was Fred pretty well, wasn't it? Six steps up and six steps down.

Katharine Hepburn

It was thrilling, thrilling, Freddy Astaire's talent. Extraordinary.

Mikhail Baryshnikov

It's no secret—we dancers hate him. He gives us complexes, because he's too perfect. His perfection is an absurdity that's hard to face. His sense of invention as a performer inspires unforgettable jealousy. When I first saw Mr. Astaire's movies, it was very discouraging. I thought everybody in America was that good, and I felt, You're never gonna dance, kid.

With Tilly Losch in *The Band Wagon*
at the New Amsterdam Theatre,
New York, 1931.

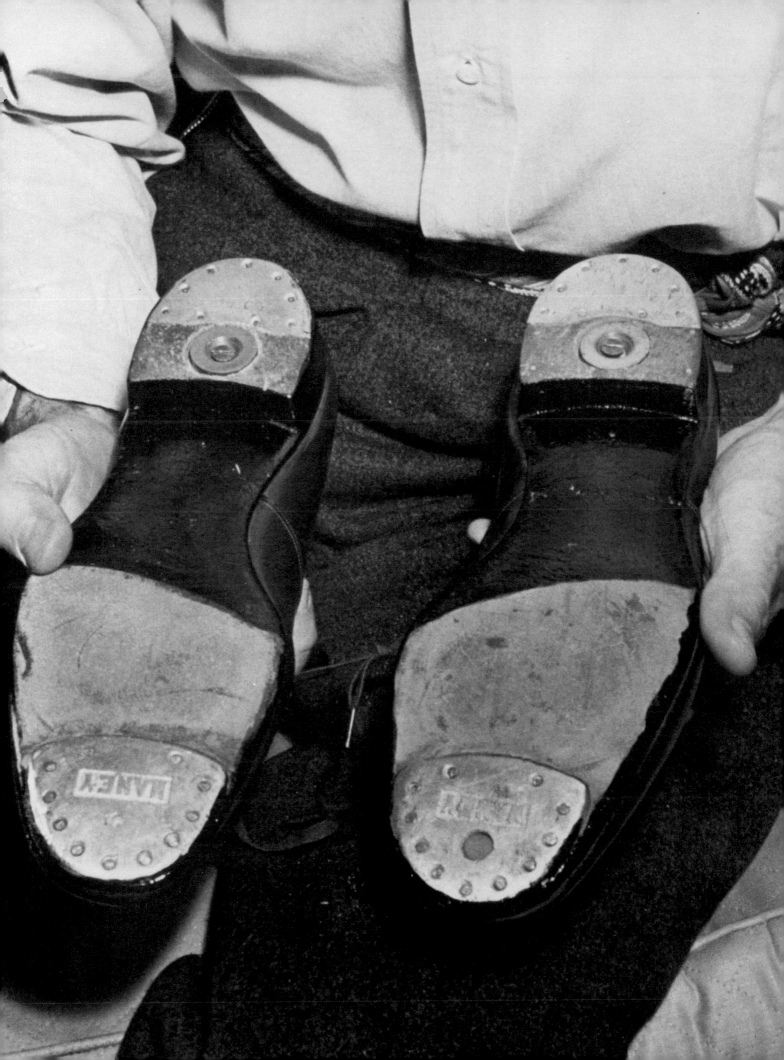

Left: Fred Astaire's tap shoes. *Above*: Wearing slippers given to him by Douglas Fairbanks, he files his taps smooth, 1941.

Dancing with, (top to bottom) Leslie Caron, Rita Hayworth, Claire Luce, Judy Garland, and Dolores Del Rio.

Lady Alexandra Metcalfe

There were other marvelous dancers in the twenties and thirties, like Jack Buchanan, but none of them had the elegance and grace of Fred. There were no ballet movements in Fred, none of those stunning things that ballet dancers do; therefore, I would have ignorantly thought that the Nureyevs and the Margots couldn't learn anything from Fred, because he elegantly moved about with his feet never far off the ground. Those ballet dancers are so muscular, and there was nothing muscular about Fred. He never had a lady tossed towards him, did he? He would whirl one away and pull her back, arms around the waist, but he never had to do anything that needed any muscle. I think it is fascinating that the ballet dancers should think he was as great as they did.

Anthony Perkins

When he did the big dance numbers in *Funny Face,* the word would go out to the offices and to the studio personnel that Fred would be doing such and such a dance at such and such a time, and suddenly there would be two hundred people who would just put their phones on hold and wander over to watch him. One such number was "Clap Yo' Hands," which he did with Kay Thompson. I remember the first assistant saying, "Okay, everybody, next door."

I was doing a Western. All these people in Western outfits were standing and watching this French party—all these gunslingers watching Fred and Kay do the number. And Fred was pleased that people would leave their other films and come and watch.

Carol Lynley

The most amazing thing about Fred is that he didn't retire from dancing until he was seventy-six. Then he said, "It hurts too much now, it just hurts too much."

Roddy McDowall

He wasn't young when he became the huge success. He was in his mid-thirties. He was a phenomenon, like Mae West.

David Bailey

When I was a kid, he was one of my three heroes. Fred Astaire, John Huston, and James Fisher, the naturalist, were the three people I wanted to be.

Jack Lemmon

Long before I worked with Fred, I'd worked with Jimmy Cagney and Hank Fonda, and, God knows, you can't worship anybody more than I did them. But there was a quality about Fred that I had never encountered before to that extent. I had found in those others that they were not affected by their fame, or by the fact that people fell over at the mention of their names. They were so absolutely engrossed professionally in their work that there was no guile, no pomposity, no conceit. But I never encountered with anyone as much as with Fred the feeling that the man had absolute greatness. There was no question about it. The man was a genius. He was alone, untouchable, and absolutely oblivious to it. I do not believe—unless maybe in his deep, deep inner thoughts—that he ever thought, My God, I'm great. I never ever felt that he felt that. And I think it's one of the reasons why he continued to be so brilliant as long as he chose to work.

Stanley Donen

The first picture I made with Fred was *Royal Wedding*. It was going to be made by another director, with Fred Astaire and Judy Garland, and the other director refused to work with Judy (he'd just done a picture with her, and it had been too difficult). It was only my second movie. I was wild with joy.

Leonard Gershe

No one must ever minimize the contribution of Hermes Pan to the legend that is Fred Astaire. His contribution was not only in the choreography but also in the humor. Fred rarely worked without Hermes. Two nights after Fred died, I watched a tape of *Roberta,* a very early one, and already there's Hermes's name. They were together forever. Both of them were very modest, shy people, so nobody ever said who did what. To my knowledge, they never argued; they just did their work. They were professional, and they set about it every day.

Irving "Swifty" Lazar

I used to watch him rehearse at Metro. It was great to see him because he varied things, stopped in the middle of something, stopped and went off. He was very inventive in his dancing. Hermes Pan was the only person he could talk to when he was doing routines. He believed in Hermes. Hermes could say anything and it would be acceptable to Fred.

Dancing with, (top to bottom) Eleanor Powell, Cyd Charisse, Joan Leslie, Ginger Rogers, and Rita Hayworth.

With George Balanchine.

Hermes Pan

I was assigned to *Flying Down to Rio* as an assistant, and Fred and Ginger weren't the stars. I was the assistant to a man named Dave Gould. My first job was to see if I could be of any help to Fred Astaire, who was rehearsing up on Stage 8. That scared the life out of me, because Fred was already a big star, a stage star—everybody had heard of Fred and Adele Astaire. I introduced myself and told him my name was Pan, which is what he always called me, not Hermes. He asked me to come in, and he said that he was just fooling around, working on a little routine. He showed me what he had and asked me what I thought so far. I told him that it was fantastic, which it was. It was wonderful. He said that he was stuck for a little break just there, and something clicked, and I showed him what I was thinking of—just a short break. He thought it was good, so he used it. And from then onwards he always called for me, never for Dave Gould, who was the dance director. (There were no choreographers in those days. The first time I ever heard the word choreographer was during *Oklahoma!*) And then they gave me a contract, and Gould was released, and I did all the rest of the Astaire work for his films. I used to dub in Ginger's taps during rehearsals.

Fred and I thought alike. This was what I'd always dreamed a dancer should be. This was the sort of dancing I loved, and I think Fred recognized a kindred spirit in me. He took my judgment a lot, but we'd disagree sometimes. I would suggest something, and he would say he didn't want to do it, and I would ask him to try it. When we were rehearsing *Let's Dance,* I suggested to him that he step over the back of a chair, or three or four, as an exit. Fred said he wouldn't do it, that he would break a leg. I begged him to try it, and still he insisted that he couldn't do it. I held his hand and he did it, and then he said, "I told you I can't do it." And we both cracked up laughing.

Audrey Hepburn

I met him when I got to Paramount, on the big, big stage, where there was just a piano and a darling choreographer named Hermes Pan. Hermes was terribly like Fred; it's unbelievable how much of Fred rubbed off on Hermes, and perhaps of Hermes on Fred. I was terribly, terribly nervous, but Fred was so easy. That's the way he seemed when he danced; there was that wonderful nonchalance. Did we practice a lot? Are you kidding? For hours, and hours, and hours, and hours, and hours. And he instantly put me at ease, by his sweetness.

**Fred Astaire and Hermes Pan
plan the dance steps for *Roberta*, 1935.**

Stanley Donen

We were recording one of the musical numbers on the recording stage with the orchestra before we shot. It was Audrey's first number with Fred, and she was very ill at ease and nervous, as anybody would be. I was in a mixing booth, and they were out on the stage, and she made a mistake, so I said, "Hold it." She said she was terribly sorry, and we started again. She made a mistake again, and this time she stopped and asked to start again. The third time we went through it, she made a mistake, and Fred jumped in and did something wrong on purpose. He said, "Oh, I'm so sorry. I've ruined it. Can we do it again?" It was so wonderful, and I'm not sure that she ever realized. He was so fabulous.

Mrs. Sammy Davis, Jr.

Sammy once did a TV special, and Fred wrote Sammy to express how he felt about it. Sammy was like a kid in a candy store. Sammy and Fred had a mutual-admiration society. When Sammy got that letter from Fred, he was ecstatic. The letter really explained what they felt for one another. It was one dancer to another. I framed it for Sammy. I once asked Fred whether he got nervous before he performed, and he answered that he always got a little bit nervous. Otherwise, he said, he wouldn't be good.

Fred Astaire, Letter to Sammy Davis, Jr.

Gotta Sing! Gotta Dance! Gotta write this note!
Dear Sammy:
Wow-e-e-e-eee! I'm still reacting to the reverberations of the magnificent "Sammy" Special Friday night. My! My! My! Man!! Brilliant! Exciting! Tasteful! Powerful and Unmatchable!
Sincerely,
Fred Astaire

Follow the Fleet, 1936.

Martha Graham

Fred had an ability to surmount form, and to seem to create at the same instant a new form, which is the mark of an intrinsic dancer. Alone or with a partner, his body was one with whatever he was performing.

Mrs. Oscar Levant

Oscar worked on *The Barkleys of Broadway*. Ginger Rogers was the second choice, and Fred and Ginger hadn't worked together for ten years. Judy Garland was supposed to be the leading lady, but she had one of her nervous breakdowns—symptoms of stage fright, a bit like Oscar's, except that Oscar always showed up. Judy had been all fitted with wardrobe, and Oscar was so excited about working with her, and then she didn't show up. Even Louis B. Mayer went to try and talk her into doing the movie, but eventually they knew they had to replace her, and they got Ginger. During one shoot, Judy showed up on the set, happy and laughing, dressed in one of the outfits she'd been fitted for, and the production stopped. She sat right next to the cameraman, watching the scene, and Ginger became very unnerved finally and retired to her dressing room. She's not the kind of person who is given to quarreling. So the production stopped, and nobody had the nerve to tell Judy to leave. But Chuck Walters, the director, had to tell Judy that Ginger had left the set and that production had to get going again. Judy began to shriek "That no-talent" and other horrible things about Ginger. Finally Chuck had to take her by the arm and lead her screaming out the door. As Chuck was leading her out, in walked Fred. He said, "What are they doing to this poor little mixed-up kid?"

Rudolf Nureyev

I met Fred Astaire in 1963, when I was with Royal Ballet in Los Angeles, but I hadn't seen any of his films yet. He was charming, very nice, but I didn't have much to say to him. What was so extraordinary about Astaire was his musicality, his agility. He was music in motion. He invented his own rhythm, he imposed his own musicality, as if he wrote another instrument into orchestration.

Dancing up a storm in *Carefree*, 1938.

13

At Versailles, *above and opposite,* dancing for the G.I.'s in a U.S.O. show, 1944

Leslie Caron

When he asked for me for *Daddy Long Legs,* I was really beside myself. I had just danced *Cinderella* with Roland Petit's company. I wasn't a hoofer, I didn't know how to tap. Fred was a fabulous partner. He didn't like ballet—ballet was a bore for him. He said to me, "My hands are so huge. Look at them. In ballet you've got to hold your hands so gracefully, and my hands are so big that I would look ridiculous." He always held his third and fourth fingers almost on top of each other to minimize the size of his hands.

Was Fred romantic? Well, there's a contradiction. Because he didn't bullshit you. He did not lay it on thick like some actors, who give you the eye and make you so embarrassed. He was a gentleman. He behaved like a gentleman. He was a fabulous partner.

Audrey Hepburn

Was he romantic? Well, *Funny Face* was a romantic movie, so the whole thing was so romantic. You get what you get from anybody who feels what he's doing, and doing it well. You catch the mood. A lot of it is unsaid and unspoken. It's all very hard to put into words. He was a very, very dear man.

Ava Astaire

Daddy wasn't a romantic, not at all. He was very enigmatic about that sort of thing. He had an amazing ability to make it seem so in films, but that was a job. He once asked my husband, "What is the story of *Romeo and Juliet?*" Richard explained that it was like *West Side Story*.

Leonard Gershe

The only dancing partner he didn't really cotton to was Kay Thompson. She's a strong woman. Now, he liked strong women, because his wife, Phyllis, was a strong woman, and his sister, Dellie, was strong, and so was his mother. But they were feminine. Kay has a mannish, direct approach to things, almost masculine—which is not to say that she is not a full woman. He was much more attracted to the femininity of Audrey Hepburn, say. With Audrey he was solicitous—he was darling, protective. She called for that, whereas Kay was a big woman. Maybe he didn't feel needed with Kay as he did with Audrey. He liked dancing with Cyd Charisse. I still think Ginger was the best.

Cyd Charisse

The first time I danced with him professionally was in a little thing called *Ziegfeld Follies*. Arthur Freed hired me, and it was the first thing I did at MGM. I had to do a little dance on point. Fred was in tails and top hat, so since I was dancing on points I didn't dance with him. I just danced around him, and I was thrilled to think that I was doing even that. Little did I know that I would be in the other films with him.

Betty Comden

My partner, Adolph Green, and I did two movies with Fred Astaire, *The Barkleys of Broadway* and *The Band Wagon*. It was very exciting, because he was someone we had worshipped when we were kids. He was the essence of everything one wanted to be. And suddenly we were writing pictures for Himself. He was a very, very hard worker. We met him one day on the lot; he was just strolling along. It was devastating. Arthur Freed always made us read our scripts to the cast, so we would have a chance to act out the whole thing. Fred would say, "Oh, well, you can't ever top that. Nothing could ever be as good as that." He was very complimentary. Fred always felt that his leading ladies were too tall for him. We wrote that into the script of *The Band Wagon*.

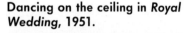

Dancing on the ceiling in *Royal Wedding*, 1951.

Sam Goldwyn, Jr.

He called me up once to congratulate me on a picture of mine which he'd just seen. He was generous with his compliments about other people. People were staggered by this part of him. The film of mine he liked so much was a black movie called *Cotton Comes to Harlem.* He knew about everything, and he liked movies and liked to see what was going on. He was very taken with Francis Coppola early on. They did *Finian's Rainbow* together. He said that Coppola still had quite a bit to learn about musicals, but that he had enormous talent.

Audrey Hepburn

Did he give me confidence? Oh yes, from the first minute. Before we actually started rehearsing the number, he said, "Come on, let's have a little go together," and we just danced around together. He just took me and turned me around, or whatever. It was such fun, it was so divine. We were laughing and having fun. Ah, it was great. I didn't feel too self-conscious, in the sense that I was meeting the great Fred Astaire. I mean, I knew I wasn't a very good dancer, so I never expected to be a great dancer. I just hoped he could deal with my lack of whatever it was, and he really did sweep it away.

I think it was Stanley Donen who had wanted the two of us for *Funny Face,* and Richard Avedon had a lot to do with it. It was greatly autobiographical, you know, about a fashion photographer, and Avedon was on the picture most of the time. He worked on the script with Leonard Gershe. Fred and I didn't spend much time together socially, because on a picture like that one got so bushed, and we had to get up early. I had to get up a lot earlier than he did, because I had all the makeup and stuff. We may have had one party on the set, I really cannot remember, but there were no dinners after work. It was such a long time ago. Oh, la la, it was thirty years ago. In a way it seems like yesterday.

Funny Face took three months. We went to Paris, and it rained—it rained a lot, very soggy. We shot in the streets and some kind of semi-interiors. And then we had that very muddy but pretty dance with me in the bridal veil. It was sheer mud we were dancing on. I had on these white satin dancing pumps made in Paris, very expensive. I had about nine pairs, because they'd get so black. My clothes were made by Givenchy. The lengths have changed— obviously a lot of things have changed—but they still look pretty good. Fred never asked me what my clothes were going to be before shooting. He was very low-key, very relaxed.

Rehearsing at the RKO Studios, 1934.

Douglas Fairbanks, Jr.

Fred was the most brilliant mimic. After seeing *Saturday Night Fever,* he became fascinated by John Travolta, and asked if he could meet him, which he duly did. Fred's imitation of Travolta had to be seen and heard to be believed, it was so good.

Mrs. Lester Holt

Fred was a terrific impersonator. One day at the track, he and I were going to get a sandwich, and I wasn't paying any attention, and all of a sudden I heard this terrific impersonation of Les. He had him down to a tee.

Mrs. Oscar Levant

One night I asked Fred if he ever watched Michael Jackson on the videos, with his terrific walk, the moonwalk. Fred said that Jackson would have to change his routine and be careful never to repeat himself in his steps. That was interesting to hear from the horse's mouth.

Twiggy

Fred was my hero—the way he dressed, the way he moved. I also loved his singing. And he was probably the most charming man I've ever met.

Leslie Caron

Fred was absolutely finicky about timing. He used to tell me how wobbly poor Ginger was. She wasn't a trained dancer, whereas he was a perfectionist. I did one number with him which we never rehearsed. We just filmed it. Fred's assistant said, "Fred will show it to you before shooting." So I went to makeup, put on my dress, and he proceeded to guide me through a whole montage—a bit of waltz, a bit of *paso doble,* a bit of cha-cha-cha. When you were in his arms, you just knew how to dance—anything. With Fred, the director always took the backseat. Everything was always Fred.

Jack Haley, Jr.

When it came time to premiere *That's Entertainment,* Adele happened to be in town. The premiere was at the Beverly Wilshire Hotel, and they had pleaded with me to put together a show. The hosts of the evening were Liza and Sammy Davis, Jr., so we bring on the Nicholas Brothers, and then Liza or Sammy got Debbie Reynolds up on stage and Saul Chaplin played piano. Debbie then gets Donald O'Connor; they in turn get Gene up on stage, and now this party starts to happen. Fifteen minutes later, there's this

With Joan Crawford.

With Ginger Rogers, in her famous

feather dress, dancing "Cheek to

Cheek" in *Top Hat,* 1935.

huge lineup doing the shim-sham, and the place is going crazy. After they finish, while Tony Martin is singing "Change Partners," the lights go down. I'm sitting with the Astaires, and I lean over to Ava and whisper, "Now, don't you worry. We're not going to make him go up there." When the lights start going up again, we see that there's no sign of Fred. There he is halfway up the stairs to the stage. He got Adele up on stage, Gene Kelly came up, they got Ginger, and Adele started dancing with Gene and Fred with Ginger. It was an amazing sight. Fred's whole point of view was "I did it, it's over. Next!"

Leonard Gershe

He was mostly interested in how he looked in the dances. In the few things I worked with him on, never once did he ask for a change in the script. Never once did he ask me to define the character, or what the motivation was. I knew how to write a line for Fred Astaire—economical, simple, easy. You couldn't make him sound Eugene O'Neillish. He wouldn't have come off right. It was fun to write for that image that you'd grown up seeing, and I knew how he should talk. He dictated to me, in other words.

Rudolf Nureyev

There's a lot of meat in his dancing. His movement is so focused that his partner—man or woman—will do the same steps. His strength comes from focusing, and this focusing may change direction, but the movement is like sun through a magnifying glass—it's concentrated to the point where it burns. There was no damned jibber-jabber about him. He had a particular genius, like Japanese theater.

Choreographically, I take from him the way I phrase, the way he moves suddenly from big outburst of tap dancing to very sublime moving, in a great swish.

Herb Ross

His sense of rhythm was impeccable, like a drummer's. His sense of time, too. He was smack on. And he never did more than he could do. He had refined what he could do to a high art, and he never tried to exceed it.

Roddy McDowall

One time I called him up because I had just seen *Broadway Melody of 1940,* the film with Eleanor Powell. He said he'd been scared to death. I asked him why. He said because she was the best, she could do everything, she was the best woman dancer probably in history. They were so polite to each other they almost couldn't dance.

Roller-skating "Let's Call the Whole Thing Off" in *Shall We Dance,* 1937.

The Duke of Devonshire

There was always gossip that Fred had lost a very great deal of money in the Fred Astaire dancing schools, which never took off.

Mrs. Oscar Levant

I remember seeing Gene Kelly and Fred Astaire soon after *That's Entertainment*. They were doing a TV special together in a large MGM studio, and there was a big buffet. Everybody who had ever worked at MGM had been invited to come, so the stage was crowded with celebrities. I saw Gene and Fred at the same moment, and their reaction was so different: Gene is very warm and outgoing, and he rushed over and threw his arms around me and gave me a big hug, but Fred walked over and very politely shook my hand and commented how nice it was to see me.

Leonard Gershe

I took him to see *A Chorus Line*. Michael Bennett knew I knew Fred, and he said he'd give me anything in the world. So Fred and I and Michael and his then wife went to dinner together, and we had a great time. We went for a drink at Fred's bar in his house, and then we went to Trader Vic's. And then a few weeks later I took Fred to see the show, and he was mad about it. I didn't want to say we should go backstage. He said it. All the dancers were so thrilled. When we left he said, "I can't understand them making such a fuss over me when I've just seen what I've seen."

Stanley Donen

I introduced Fred to Bob Fosse when Bob was a very young dancer. He was making a picture with me at MGM. Bob naturally admired Fred enormously, and once when we were walking down a street at MGM, we saw Fred coming toward us. Fosse was flabbergasted. I introduced them, and both of them shyly looked at the ground. There was a lot of stuttering and stammering, and Fred said, "Well, I'd better be going." Now, there was a little nail on the ground right at his feet, and he went *zap!* with his foot, and the nail went sailing off like a gunshot—*ting!*—and then he walked away. Fosse was bewildered at this agility. Nobody else would ever have kicked a nail like that.

Mikhail Baryshnikov

You remember the remark by Ilie Nastase about Bjorn Borg? He said, "We are playing tennis. He's playing something else." It's the same with Fred Astaire. We are dancing, but he's doing something else.

Top hat, white tie, and tails.

HIS ENERGY AND PERFECTIONISM

In *Blue Skies*, 1946.

Everyone who ever worked with Fred talks about his tireless insistence on perfection. Alone, or with Hermes Pan, his longtime choreographer, or with any of his long succession of stunning partners, he would rehearse a routine until he got it right, regardless of whether it took a hundred repetitions or a thousand. He would struggle with the hardest dance sequences until they looked simple, and he refused to take shortcuts or to settle for easy solutions. He would only be filmed full figure, head to toe, with as few cuts as possible. Unlike classical ballet dancers, Fred never repeated himself; he had no repertoire to fall back on. As a result, he forced himself to be endlessly creative, always fiddling, always experimenting, with a chair, or an umbrella, or any other prop at hand. The most amazing thing of all about him was that he didn't consider his extraordinary output as being in any way more laudable or remarkable than the best work of any other conscientious craftsman. As he once put it, "We just went to work on Monday."

On the set of *The Barkleys of Broadway*, 1949.

Michael Jackson

I could only repeat what has been said and written about Fred Astaire's perfectionism and enormous, one-of-a-kind artistry. What I can reflect on is the inspiration he afforded me personally, being privileged as I was to see him work his magic. Nobody could duplicate Mr. Astaire's ability, but what I never stop trying to emulate is his total discipline, his absolute dedication to every aspect of his art. He rehearsed, rehearsed, and rehearsed some more, until he got it just the way he wanted it. It was Fred Astaire's work ethic that few people ever discussed and even fewer could ever hope to equal.

Hermes Pan

He had tremendous stamina, and seemed to be able to go on forever. His energy was amazing. We'd call each other in the middle of the night with ideas.

Leslie Caron

He was perfectly formed for dancing. The sinews within were quick, he was just the right height, and there was the right metabolism, the right balance between his heartbeat and glands—which makes you fast or slow. He had this incredible speed and tremendous nervous energy, and a remarkable breathing capacity. When I danced with him, he was fifty-five, and he would go through a whole number, and at the end of it he would go, *"Ugh."* At the end of "Sluefoot," which lasted seven minutes—and we moved as fast as possible—he just went, *"Ugh,"* whereas I was totally out of breath.

Liza Minnelli

I remember him in the rehearsal hall, or in my dad's living room. He was just a friend of my dad—by that time my mom had left the studio. I used to sit and watch him for hours, and I noticed how hard he worked, until he'd worked every little detail out. That stuck with me. That's why I have the rehearsal habits I have, which drive people crazy because they're minute. I think I picked it up from watching the way Fred worked.

Left and opposite: 1936, the year of Swing Time.

Roddy McDowall

He knew how to conserve himself. In movies, you have to conserve your energy, because you never know what time of the day or night you will have to be doing the scene. In Fred's case, for instance, in the RKO days, a lot of his scenes were done at one o'clock in the morning. He had to pace himself like a racehorse. When Fred and I were making *The Midas Run,* we shot some of it on an airfield somewhere outside Milan. It was very hot, and Fred was playing an Englishman from the government, pinstripes and all that. Suddenly I would look around, and it was adorable: There was Fred in a straightback chair, sitting under the wing of a big airplane. It was the only shade, and he sat in it dead upright, napping. He knew exactly how to recharge.

Sam Goldwyn, Jr.

Pan always says how precise Fred was about detail, and Fred used to give Pan credit for being a very hard taskmaster. They were working dancers, just like Picasso was a working artist. I once asked Fred how he developed a number, and he just shrugged and said, "Oh, I don't know. Pan and I sort of talk about it together and try to figure it out, and Hermes sort of puts it together and I sort of do it—you know, it's a job of work." I always thought that the golf-ball number in *A Damsel in Distress* with Joan Fontaine was one of the great numbers, and when I told Fred this, he said, "It works, doesn't it? It took a lot of time to do that."

Nancy Reagan

Fred and I were at Metro-Goldwyn-Mayer at the same time, but unfortunately I never worked with him or knew him well. I don't think many people did. However, everyone on the lot knew about him—what a perfectionist he was, how he would work for months rehearsing a dance sequence until he got it down just right.

Jamie Niven

Fred was very meticulous. He always had a new Cadillac, and it was always in the shop because it always had to be in perfect shape, as though it had been tuned the day before. The balance had to be just right. I'm sure the car was more in the shop than out. Fred brought to his life the same perfectionism that he had on screen. He could do so many "first takes" because he was so well rehearsed.

Mrs. Oscar Levant

Oscar had a coronary just before *The Band Wagon.* He was totally immobilized, and he was a real hypochondriac. He was supposed to walk down this big ramp in the opening of *That's Entertainment,* and he said his doctor didn't want him to do it. Fred said, "But you've got to. You're in the number. I mean, for God's sake, Oscar, I'll carry you down." He said it very disgustedly, so Oscar did it.

David Niven, Jr.

Anybody who danced with him was made to go over the steps time and time and time again. Your feet were bleeding by the time Fred was done. It's a shame they don't make them like that anymore; they broke the mold.

Jack Haley, Jr.

I first met Fred through Dave Robell. Dave was a technician, and vital to Fred. He was the one who laid down Fred's taps. He'd go into the sound studio with Fred, and they would work out the taps. Fred was always so loyal to guys like Dave. He was such a perfectionist.

Stanley Donen

When we were rehearsing *Funny Face* with Audrey, Fred was dancing at one point with the umbrella, and I said, "Why don't we open the umbrella and see what happens? Let's see if there are any moves." So he opened the umbrella and danced around a bit, and after a little while he closed the umbrella, and suddenly he rolled the umbrella up the way he does in the movie, and it was the most fantastic thing I've ever seen. I said, "Fred, how did you do that?" And he said, "I've practiced it." And that's the point: He would practice things that didn't have any immediate connection with anything.

Ava Astaire

Being a perfectionist is what drove Daddy to work so hard, I think. I worked as production assistant on the television shows he did with Barrie Chase. Ours were the only shows in those days that had at least six weeks of rehearsal. Most shows had only a couple of weeks' rehearsal. Daddy and Pan had to get the extra rehearsal time because Daddy felt it was necessary.

Jack Lemmon

He approached everything first as a worrier. He worked like a demon. Talk about perfectionism—my God almighty, he was the greatest taskmaster on himself that I have ever seen in my life. We did a two-hour special on George and Ira Gershwin's music a couple of years ago, and I was the emcee. There was a section where Fred did excerpts from six or seven songs that the Gershwins had written for him. It was all solo. He would go through them, and from the first take on, it was flabbergasting, it was stupendous, all these incredible songs, one after another, written specifically for him by the Gershwins. The studio was empty except for the technicians and Fred and me. The director was in the control booth. Fred and I would sit side by side, on two stools in front of a monitor, and watch Fred's stuff played back over and over. Nobody in the world could have found a frame that wasn't just gorgeous, and wonderful, the singing and the dancing. But Fred would say over and over, "I didn't like that inflection. That turn wasn't right." He was not concerned with what other people would think; he was satisfying himself. Now, that kind of seeming selfishness is what makes a great performer. I said to him, "God, Fred, what does it feel like to realize that the Gershwins sat down and wrote all these songs specifically for you to perform? That must be an incredible feeling." And he said, "Huh?" and he looked at me and thought for a second, and then he said, "Berlin wrote more." He said it with complete, direct honesty. It was just a fact.

Bob Mackie

I worked with Fred on the television special which he did in 1968. He always knew what he wanted to look like, and he was very particular about every detail. I was in my twenties, and I would sit in rehearsals and we would talk it over and over. I never did a show in which they rehearsed so much. I thought I would never finish that project, although I loved it the whole time. I used to watch him at the mirror, rehearsing the little talk that he did at the beginning of the show. He wouldn't just rehearse the words, he would rehearse how his hand went in his pocket, and how he would stand with just his thumb out, and how he would hold his hands in just a certain way. This was during lunch, when he wasn't working on the dance parts. When I watch him now, I realize how rehearsed his hands were. He was very conscious of his large hands. If he'd had them just flapping around, they would have seemed huge, so, like a dancer, he always planned where they were going to be. He was small in every other way, very slight, but with a big head and big hands.

Herb Ross

Fred asked me to do his last television show. On the first day of rehearsal, my wife, Nora Kay and I sat there with him, staring at one another for what seemed like an eternity. We started with "Limehouse Blues," and I showed him the steps, which I am sure he had done a thousand times before. He exclaimed, "How wonderful, how fresh!" Later I asked him why there had been a tenseness before we got dancing, and he said it was because he thought that Nora was such a great and such an extraordinary artist that he felt intimidated and clumsy. The dancers' call was for ten in the morning, and he would come by eight and do a couple of hours before the others arrived, so that he was always warmed up and had rehearsed all the new material. We rehearsed eight weeks on that show, which was unprecedented for a television show. He was very slow, and it took him a lot of time to achieve that totally dégagé, spontaneous feeling. It really was a result of getting all the movements into the muscle. Memory is muscular, so if you do a movement enough times, it's in the muscle.

Mrs. Sammy Davis, Jr.

When I'd ask him if he was ever going to dance again, go back on the stage, or do a special for television, he would say, "No, no. It takes so long. I have to rehearse for months in advance." He wouldn't just rehearse for two weeks; he had to make sure everything was perfect. Every line was a picture, so he decided he wouldn't do any more.

Roddy McDowall

He had three separate movie careers—or four, if you count the TV career. RKO, Paramount, and MGM. Even five careers if you count the stage one. Plus the fact that he was a very appealing actor, which he never thought. He enjoyed working.

Carol Lynley

I made Fred read the Arlene Croce book about Ginger and him, and he noticed a couple of mistakes. So he called her up and pointed them out. In the second printing, she corrected the mistakes. So I warn you to get your facts right, because he'll come right down and strike you. He was very sweet about that, but very strict. He liked things just right.

1933, the year of *Dancing Lady* and *Flying Down to Rio*.

GINGER ROGERS

With Ginger Rogers in *Swing Time*,
1936.

After Fred and Adele broke up as a dancing team, he never anticipated having another steady partner. Less than a year later, however, he was cast for the first time with blond, vivacious Ginger Rogers. Although Ginger may not have had the technical genius of Eleanor Powell, or the extraordinary beauty of Rita Hayworth, or the long legs of Cyd Charisse, or the balletic expertise of Leslie Caron, or the elasticity of Barrie Chase, or the fragile charm of Audrey Hepburn, she proved to be the one with whom he consistently made magic. Between 1933 and 1939, they made nine films together; they teamed up again in 1949 for The Barkleys of Broadway. Their best numbers, over the years, are without doubt the towering peaks of the movie musical—"The Carioca," "The Yam," "The Continental," "The Castle Walk," "Cheek to Cheek," "Change Partners," "Let's Call the Whole Thing Off," "Let's Face the Music and Dance."

During and after Ginger's dancing days with Fred, she was also a stunning and versatile actress in dramatic films. She gave Katharine Hepburn a run for her money in Stage Door in 1937, for instance, and won an Oscar for best actress in 1940 for Kitty Foyle.

Fred Astaire and Ginger Rogers, 1939.

Hermes Pan

He got along with Ginger perfectly, and I get so mad
hearing the same old baloney, because I never heard the
two of them having one cross word. I do not think that
Eleanor Powell was Fred's greatest dancing partner. I think
Ginger Rogers was. Not that she was the greatest of the
dancers. Cyd Charisse was a much finer technical dancer.
But there was something when Fred and Ginger danced
which was magic. They seemed to go together.

Stanley Donen

I don't think there's ever been anyone like Ginger, never.
She was heaven. She wasn't anything like a great dancer,
but she was good enough to look feminine and sweet and
receptive and matching.

Lady Alexandra Metcalfe

Fred was so graceful that you frankly watched him and not
Ginger Rogers—that's not very complimentary to Ginger
Rogers, but your eyes could not leave Fred.

**With Ginger Rogers in *Flying Down
to Rio*, 1933.**

Douglas Fairbanks, Jr.

Ginger was a simple girl, an ex–chorus girl. She was not worldly. She did not move in that world of society in London, New York, and Paris that Fred moved in. Ginger went straight from New York shows to Hollywood films, and she never had any friends, that I knew of, outside that world. So Fred and Ginger never really had anything in common.

Ginger Rogers

Well, I think when you work with somebody all day long, for ten movies, you become good friends, though he was as delighted not to see me at night over dinner as I was.

Dominick Dunne

I got to know Ginger when I was the stage manager on a live TV spectacular in the late fifties. It was *Tonight at 8:30*, the Noël Coward thing, directed by Otto Preminger, with Ginger in four different parts. I got to know her very well. She and Fred were never friends. I mean, they weren't pals, they weren't soulmates. I think it was a slightly snob thing. Ginger was never in the same set, shall we say?

Ava Astaire

Daddy never had any feuding thing with her—they were just not particular friends. She was just different from Daddy. When Ginger won the Oscar for *Kitty Foyle*, Daddy sent her a telegram that said simply, "Ouch," which was lovely.

Slim Keith

I think there was a little more than rehearsal. Maybe there was a flirt, I don't know. There wouldn't have been any more than that—it would never have been anything consummated. I just always felt that kind of an electric thing that's there, that you kind of know.

With Ginger Rogers in *The Story of Vernon and Irene Castle*, 1939. Below, Fred, aged eighty-three, and Ginger, aged seventy-two, in 1982.

Mark Sandrich, Ginger Rogers, Fred Astaire, and Irving Berlin outside an RKO sound studio during the filming of *Top Hat*, 1935.

With Barrie Chase on a TV special.

Although Fred knew Barrie Chase as a child, it wasn't until 1957 that he discovered her as a brilliant young dance talent. After seeing her rehearse on the film set of Les Girls, he got her a small part in Silk Stockings. They went on to make four TV specials over the next ten years, and the first one alone, An Evening with Fred Astaire, won nine Emmys. Fred was more than a Pygmalion to Barrie. She was thought to be his favorite partner, and his friends believed that, despite an age difference of at least thirty-five years, the two of them might even marry.

Right and overleaf: **Rehearsing with Barrie Chase, September 1960.**

With Barrie Chase on a TV special.

Rehearsing with Barrie Chase,
September 1960.

Bob Mackie

Barrie Chase was his partner on the 1968 television special, and her dresses were so short. Fred liked that, because she had great legs. He loved Barrie. She was a wonderful dancer, and a very modern, stylish kind of a girl, not your Hollywood starlet type at all. She would always have the latest haircut. She was an interesting girl for him to choose to dance with, and it made him seem very modern. If he'd gone for a latter-day Ginger Rogers, nobody would have said anything, but it wouldn't have been the same. Barrie was so current. The last time I saw her, she was all done up in Japanese clothes. Barrie had the latest in everything. She had that kind of mentality.

Slim Keith

When his wife Phyllis died, he went into almost total retreat. One never saw him at all. Then he began to work with another girl regularly, Barrie Chase, whom everyone though he was going to marry, but he didn't. The television show they did together was not great, but pretty good.

Carol Lynley

He liked Leslie Caron very much, and Barrie of course. He'd known Barrie as a child. It was little Barrie. He was a friend of her father's.

Bill Self

He used to date a lot in those days, before he married Robyn—never very seriously. He and Barrie Chase were very fond of each other.

Peter Duchin

His favorite dancer was Barrie Chase. She was also his girlfriend.

Ava Astaire

Daddy and Barrie worked beautifully together, and she's still one of my very good friends.

Hermes Pan

He liked Barrie Chase's dancing very much. He thought she was a beautiful mover.

Stanley Donen

He had a craze for Barrie, but I never worked with them. I think the one he liked to dance with most was Barrie.

HIS CLOTHES AND STYLE

Without being a clotheshorse, Fred Astaire was the most elegant dresser of his time. He could wear a suit from Savile Row's Anderson & Sheppard and a cowboy shirt from Woolworth's with equal flair. His small quirks became international trends—the necktie worn as a belt, the brightly colored socks, the English tailoring, the porkpie hat, the pleated gray flannels, the silk handkerchief around his neck. It was not just the clothes he wore, it was the way he carried himself in everyday life, the very way he walked. To even the most casual observer, Fred Astaire has "swellegance." He was hardly conventionally good-looking, but his charm was unique, even though he himself refused to see it. He hated to look at his rushes, because he thought he was funny-looking, and all his life he made no secret of his endless search for the perfect toupee to conceal his thinning hair.

In Prince of Wales tweed jacket, 1941.

Liza Minnelli

When I first started to be able to afford to dress properly, I went to Halston, and he said, "Well, what do you want to look like?" And I said, "During the day I want to look like Fred Astaire, and at night I want to look like a movie star."

Slim Keith

Fred had such a marvelous body; there wasn't an ounce of anything on him that shouldn't have been there. He could put on anything, and if it was too big around the waist, he could put a necktie around to hold his trousers up. Or a piece of string, or a piece of rope, or whatever he could find. He had it, that's all. He had something that very few men have (Bill Paley had it)—he was not just the best-dressed, but he had a manner of wearing his clothes as though he had no clothes on at all. They seemed just accidental. He had, therefore, an ease, a perfection, that was just marvelous. I don't think he ever had any idea he was setting a style; it was just how he liked to look. He used that look in films a lot; in any casual sort of scene, he was always the best casually dressed man.

David Niven, Jr.

He could't get into a bad or an awkward position, not even if he was sitting on the floor or curled up on a couch. He was a lesson in how to move.

Jeanne Vanderbilt

Fred had the most beautiful walk. Even when we were walking around the racetrack, or in the paddock, I couldn't take my eyes off the way he walked.

Nancy Reagan

He was, I think, a very shy man, kind, modest, and truly elegant in every sense of the word. I loved to just sit and just watch him walk across the screen. Our son, Ron, once interviewed him and came away with the same impression.

**Patriotic socks, belt, and cravat, in
Holiday Inn, 1942.**

Molly Keane

Fred moved directly, and with as much purpose and as little fuss as a flying bird.

Rocky Converse

Fred used to take a lot of photographs, and so did I, and we went to the same camera store on Rodeo Drive. More than once, at ten-thirty in the morning, I would be parking my car in the parking lot, and I would see Fred. I would just sit and watch him walk. It was absolute poetry. No wonder Baryshnikov and all those Ruskies say that he is America's greatest dancer. I certainly think he was.

Leonard Gershe

I think Fred's classiness was innate, because he came from Nebraska.

Carol Lynley

He developed an inner-ear infection when he was eighty-four, and it made him feel very giddy. He had a right point of view—he was definitely to the right of the world—but he wasn't really a political person. His inner-ear infection made it difficult for him to turn to the left, because he got dizzy, and I used to say, "Fred, you were never one to go that way anyway."

Sam Goldwyn, Jr.

Remember how he walked? He always had his hand in his pocket, and the pants were a little short so that you could see the stockings, so that you could see the feet.

Aboard the S.S. *Berengaria,*
September 1932.

45

Dr. Harry Reizner

Who took care of those famous feet? I did, all those years, and I kept them in good shape except when he bumped a toe or tore a ligament or pulled a muscle. The first time I met Fred Astaire was when he came to see me with an ingrown toenail. His big toe had ballooned up, and he couldn't walk, couldn't put his shoe on. So he came walking in with one shoe on. The other foot was in a slipper, cut out in front. It reminded me of the Katzenjammer Kids, the cartoon. I said, "You're limping. I thought you'd dance in." And he said, "Well, I hope to dance out." He had a nice dull sense of humor. I removed the section of the nail that had penetrated the flesh and dressed it, and he shook my hand and said, "You're a real gentleman." He had to walk with his cut-out slipper for a few days, but we had it cleared up. Then Fred became a regular patient, and I took care of his feet from then on. He had a standing appointment once a month. He'd come in at eight-thirty in the morning. He'd park his car about two blocks away, on the other side of Santa Monica Boulevard, and he'd walk the rest of the way. Then, after he'd leave here, he'd go to the post office. Thank goodness his feet were in good condition.

Until 1946 he always wore shoes that didn't fit him. They pressed on the little toe and on the big toe. This would pinch them together, and that is how he got the ingrown toenail. I suggested to him that he give himself an extra eighth of an inch. He looked at me and smiled and said, "Maybe you're right." It took me two years to convince him. His feet looked neat when they were small, and he was a neat person. One day I took his shoe and put my hydraulic stretcher in it. I put the shoe-stretching solution on it, and when he put the shoe on he said how much better it felt. And from then on, whenever he got new shoes, he got them a little rounder in the front. He used to have them made in England. Then a representative from Alan Macafie would come to Hollywood twice a year. They made shoes for Louis B. Mayer, Samuel Goldwyn, and many stars. I took care of the feet of all the heads of the studios. I took care of Howard Hughes when he took over RKO. Ginger Rogers, Cyd Charisse, and Eleanor Powell were all my patients. I give my patients a solution with menthol, which has a cooling effect on the feet. I used to have to see that Fred didn't pull his socks on too tight, especially after they'd been washed.

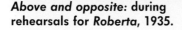

Above and opposite: during rehearsals for *Roberta,* 1935.

The quintessential English look.

Opposite, top
to bottom:
In an Anderson & Sheppard suit.

Arriving in Paris, June 1956, to film
Funny Face.

Arriving in England, August 1936, to
visit his sister, Adele, Lady Charles
Cavendish.

Ava Astaire

He bought a lot of shoes in Ireland. He thought Ireland had terrific shoes. We were in the middle of a conversation one day in Beverly Hills, and he looked down at my husband's shoes and said, "You're a sneaky dresser, Richard," because he took a fancy to Richard's shoes. He got a lot of his shoes at Carroll's in Beverly Hills. It's a nice, conservative men's store. The last present I gave him, for his last birthday, was a pair of slippers from Carroll's.

Lily Guest

Fred was always fingering his tie, which I guess he did in the movies.

Carol Lynley

He had very strong hands, truly pianist's hands. In real life he never alluded to his hands, but in interviews he used to say how he liked to hide them, because of their size. Even though he didn't look like a truck driver, he was very masculine.

Peter Duchin

I saw him once at Mrs. Whitney's daughter's house, Lowy's house—she's married to Ron Wilford, the head of Columbia Artists. Lowy told me that when Fred got up to shake her hand, she thought he was going to ask her to dance, just from the way he got up. He was a major graceful man. Balanchine had a natural grace about him, but I've never seen anybody quite like Astaire. Compare him to Gene Kelly? I mean, forget it. It's a totally different thing.

Audrey Hepburn

He had style. His clothes were always very casual, and terribly, extremely elegant, because he had such taste. Was he good-looking? I think so, because charm is the best-looking thing in the world, isn't it? Perhaps his face was too narrow and too long, but he was so chic and so stylish. Nobody could ever have had such style as Fred Astaire— not just in his face or his head, in every part of him. It was his feet and his hands, his whole body, no?

Jean Howard

Fred was a very attractive man—not like Cary Grant, not those looks, but more attractive.

H.R.H. Princess Alexandra

He had a very nice face—just like his pictures.

Jack Haley, Jr.

After watching a section of *Broadway Melody of 1940,* Cary Grant whispered to me, "Who do you think did Fred's clothes?" Cary had just gone crazy over the white tuxedo that Fred wore. There was Cary, one of the great fashion figures in all of Hollywood, asking where Fred got his clothes.

Ahmet Ertegun

I happened to be at a party where I met a young lady who was a wardrobe mistress for many top films, and she told me she was working on a television film with Fred Astaire. I told her how much I admired him, and she asked me to come out and visit the set. So I went. Now, I'd always thought that he must have the best tailors in the world and that he must be very, very careful about matching what he wore. Well, he said that he wanted to wear something different for the scene he was about to film. There was an old trunk with a lot of clothes thrown in helter-skelter, and he just picked out a pair of trousers and tried them on, and he picked up a jacket at random, and the minute he put them on he looked great. They hadn't been folded or anything—they were literally thrown in this trunk. The clothes were quickly pressed and they looked like the best Anderson & Sheppard suit you've ever seen. Actually, the jacket and trousers didn't even match. He looked fabulous. He always had great shoes. He often wore suede shoes with gray flannels, and a little foulard around his neck.

Carol Lynley

About two or three years ago, I was at Kirk and Ann Douglas's house for dinner and Dinah Shore was on one side of Cary Grant, and his wife, Barbara, was on the other, and Lee Remick and her husband were there. Cary was wearing an old blue work shirt, and it was torn at the elbows. Well, Fred was sort of like that. For his club in New York—I think it was the Brook Club—it would be pinstripes. But it was always elegance and style.

Stanley Donen

Fred didn't think of himself as romantic in the male-female sense. He was very nervous about showing any physical contact with a woman, and he thought of himself as physically unattractive. He didn't like to look at himself on screen, and he didn't like to hear himself sing. One day, after shooting, I suggested we look at the rushes, and he said, "No, I don't want to look at them. I look like a plucked chicken." He just didn't like the way he looked.

The year of *Let's Dance*, 1950.

Bob Mackie

I learned from him a little lesson that I always remember: When you see people in tails and a waistcoat, if the white hangs down under the black jacket you know they have really ruined the line of the whole outfit. Fred Astaire always wore his waistcoat very high, and the jacket would just cover the white, which of course made his legs go on forever. Nowadays when I see someone with the white showing below, I realize that it makes you look fatter and cuts you off around the middle, and it makes your legs look short. Not that Fred ever had to worry about looking fat. That was just a rule he had always known. If you watch films from the thirties, tails were always like that, but later on tails became an obsolete thing, and people didn't know how to wear them properly. That was a little lesson that he taught me, and it stayed with me. People hate me because I insist that the black jacket should cover the white waistcoat by at least half an inch, so that even if they raise their arm they have a little leeway there.

Lady Alexandra Metcalfe

Fred particularly admired the Prince of Wales's white waistcoat lapels, and also how the waistcoat did not show below the dress-coat front. When he discovered that Hawes & Curtis made the Prince of Wales's dress shirts and waistcoats, he rushed there the following morning. He also had shirts made at Beale and Inman. His suits were made by Anderson & Sheppard.

Liza Minnelli

There was a whole set of people in New York who were really under the influence of the Duke of Windsor—the way they dressed, the elegance, the spiffiness, pressed pleats, casual, easy. They were all friends of the Duke of Windsor, and I think they brought that style to Hollywood. Hollywood didn't really have that kind of elegance until this whole group of people moved out there—the Gershwins, my dad, Fred Astaire, Vernon Duke, Cole Porter . . .

Herb Ross

We made Fred's last television show in 1968, and Simon and Garfunkel were guests on it. That was when everybody was growing lots of hair and mustaches and wearing love beads—slightly psychedelic, everybody slightly stoned, before it all went sour. Fred was fascinated by all that, and he used to wear beads to rehearsal. He did indeed.

Jerry Hall

Mick Jagger and I met Fred Astaire with President Carter, at this Kennedy Center do, when Fred was given an award. He was charming and very sweet. And Mick told him how thrilled he was to meet him, and Fred said how thrilled he was to meet Mick. He had on a wonderful suit, really beautifully cut, and he looked so elegant. He was quite old, but he didn't look old. He was very sprightly on his feet, and really graceful. He slid.

Betty Comden

He always looked elegant—in the most casual sweater, or a sweatshirt, with a towel around his neck. He had that jaunty stride that nobody else has.

Sam Goldwyn, Jr.

Up to the end of his life, he used to get his hair cut at the Beverly Hills Hotel. When he didn't wear his toupee, he always wore a hat. And enormously loud socks, which would draw your eyes to his feet, which were his thing. I used to run into Brooks Brothers in New York, where I'd buy him socks—very bright socks, red or yellow.

Audrey Hepburn

I have a divine photograph of Fred. He always used to wear gray flannels. So when I asked for a photograph of him, and he signed this one and gave it to me, I had a frame made for it covered in gray flannel.

Bob Mackie

Nobody ever looked better than Fred Astaire. He wore his own blazer and his own wonderful pleated pants and his yellow shirt and the tie around the waist. He just had so much style. Anyone else could wear the exact same clothes and wouldn't look nice. He absolutely loved the brown wool Edwardian outfit he wore for one scene in the TV special. It was wool, with a belt and a velvet collar.

Leslie Caron

I used to meet him in a gentlemen's clothes shop in Beverly Hills, and the way he swung in was like watching a number—the way he walked was already like dancing. He dressed like an English gentleman. Fred didn't wear his toupee for rehearsals.

Arriving at Southampton, England, August 1932.

Henry Herbert, the Earl of Pembroke

Dominick Dunne took me to a party at Edie Goetz's in Hollywood, and I spotted Fred Astaire across the room. He was my absolute hero, so I went up to him and introduced myself. I was wearing a wonderful broad mauve tie from Rupert Lycett Green's shop, of Savile Row, Blades. Fred Astaire admired it enormously and asked me where I got it. When I got back to London, I immediately asked Rupert if he could make me a tie identical to mine, and I sent it to Fred. A few years later, I bought a pair of Fred's shoes at a sale at Christie's. I have them in a glass box at Wilton.

Don Cook

One day Ava had a garage sale, and included in the sale was a blue pinstripe suit from *The Band Wagon*. She encouraged me to buy it. I asked how much. Ava said ten dollars. I said okay and bought it. I gave it to Sammy Davis, Jr., for his birthday, and Sammy almost died.

Douglas Fairbanks, Jr.

One night my wife, Mary Lee, and I had dinner with Fred in a restaurant in New York. We noticed that he was spending a lot of time with his head bent right over his soup. Finally we asked if there was something wrong with the soup. Still with his head bent right down, he muttered, "Can't you notice anything?" "No," we said. "Oh, dear, I'm disappointed. I've got a new toupee and I wondered if it showed."

Carol Lynley

One night he rings me up and says, "I've done it, I've finally gotten it right. Come to the house right away." I get up there and he's sitting in the bar, which had a spotlight. He's behind the bar, and he turns to the spotlight and says, "Well, what do you think? The toupee?" I said, "Fred, it seems great. Very good." He said, "It's taken me over forty years to get it right, and all you can say is 'Very good'?" He put his head down and we went over the toupee, for hairline. He was always working on it, perfecting it. I never saw him without a toupee.

Stanley Donen

He would have given anything to have had hair.

Ava Astaire

He had some pretty funny clothes. When people would ask him where he got his cowboy shirt, he said from the dime store in Beverly Hills. He loved to potter around the old Newberry's five-and-ten in Beverly Hills and look for chains that he could sew onto his shoes, and diamond earrings that he could clip on his slippers—just a little glittery something.

Irving "Swifty" Lazar

He was quite tight. He'd have suits from the forties redone as late as the seventies—have the wide lapels made narrower. He just didn't want to buy new suits. He looked good in high hat and tailcoats because he was thin; he had a good body for clothes.

Stanley Donen

Everybody used to think he had special tailors, but he'd go and buy things everywhere, anywhere—a lot of clothes from Carroll's in Beverly Hills, or he'd buy off stands. He'd see something and just buy it. Then he'd get it fixed to suit his wishes. He constantly worked out his clothing and attire. He cared about how he looked.

Richard McKenzie

When Ava and I moved to London, he asked me whether I had a warm coat. "No," I said, "but I'll get one." Fred gave me the coat in which he sang "A Fine Romance" with Ginger Rogers. It had a mink collar and was fur-lined. I kept it for a bit and then gave it to a museum. Fred would have got rid of it. He had no nostalgia. He was such a current man.

Howard W. Koch

Fred always wore his porkpie hat at the races.

Tina Sinatra

He was always impeccably dressed—the ascot tie, the tie around the waist, the hat and trench coat.

Hermes Pan

Fred had a great knack for dressing, a flair—not gaudy, just a touch. He used to have white shoes with black edges around the soles, which looked very chic. His ties were always the right color, and his coats were never extreme. I think his whole style was English. He would have things sent over from England. He used to get his clothes made at Anderson & Sheppard. Sometimes the movie people would wonder if he didn't look too English; they wondered if they shouldn't Americanize him a little.

Fred Astaire at fifty-nine. "I'm limber and active without working at it. I never diet and I hate calisthenics—they bore me to death."

George Christy

I got to know Fred Astaire initially some years ago, when I was assigned an article on the way he dressed. Of course, we all loved the way he looked in movies. He and Cary Grant just had that image. Fred was in New York, and I went to visit him at the St. Regis Hotel, where he was staying. His press agent was there, and was very excited about the article, because it seemed made in heaven for Fred. I was not asking him about any illegitimate children, or wives that he'd hated—just clothes. I told him that the world was very interested to know how he'd got this terrific style—the dandy on screen, the impeccable suits. He answered, "I don't like clothes." I said, "But this cannot be." He said, "I don't know why that gets talked about; it's just not me." I realized that we were going nowhere; the interview was dead. So I tried talking about other things— seeing if maybe I could warm him up and then go back to clothes. All I got out of him was "You want to know how I feel about clothes? I just take a new suit and roll it into a ball and throw it against the wall, and that way it becomes an old suit overnight. That's how I feel about clothes." I felt strongly that he was putting me on. I think he felt that it wasn't right or nice for a man to be talking about this subject, and he was in his mid-sixties and in those days men weren't as openly clothes-conscious as they are today. He just chilled the whole idea. But he didn't fool me. We all know what a beautifully dressed man Fred Astaire was. He was always a bit standoffish after that.

Danvi Janssen

My late husband, David, and Fred Astaire went to the same little Italian tailor in Beverly Hills, up on Little Santa Monica. One day David went in to pick up a new suit, and there was Fred. The tailor comes out of the back room with Fred's new suit on a hanger and hands it to Fred. Fred takes the suit off the hanger, rolls it up, and throws it against the wall. David said, "What are you doing?" And Fred answered, "The way to wear clothes is to tell them who's boss in the beginning. Then they fit you." David always said that as long as Fred Astaire went to his tailor, he would never change.

Jeremy Tree

He was wonderfully elegant, an Anglophile, always very smart. Gray flannel trousers and tweed coats. And he really did always wear the famous tie around his waist.

Strolling in Beverly Hills in the late 1930s.

Douglas Fairbanks, Jr.

My father used to wear a tie around his waist instead of a belt—Fred just made it famous. The turned-up trousers were more particular to Fred. His style was a studied carelessness.

Alfred Vanderbilt

I don't think he was elegant; he managed to make clothes look very well. He would have looked great in what I'm wearing now, whereas I look like a slob. He loved to wear button-down sweaters, short-sleeved cardigans.

Leonard Gershe

He couldn't make an inelegant move—almost like a male Babe Paley. You could put her in a T-shirt and dungarees, and you still couldn't take it away from her. It was elegance bred in the bones. Fred had it, too.

Bob Mackie

He wore a full set of long underwear under all his costumes when he danced. It absorbed the perspiration. And of course it never made any extra bulk, because there wasn't any there. They were cotton long johns with a top, all in one piece.

In the trademark gray flannels and black-and-white shoes, August 1941.

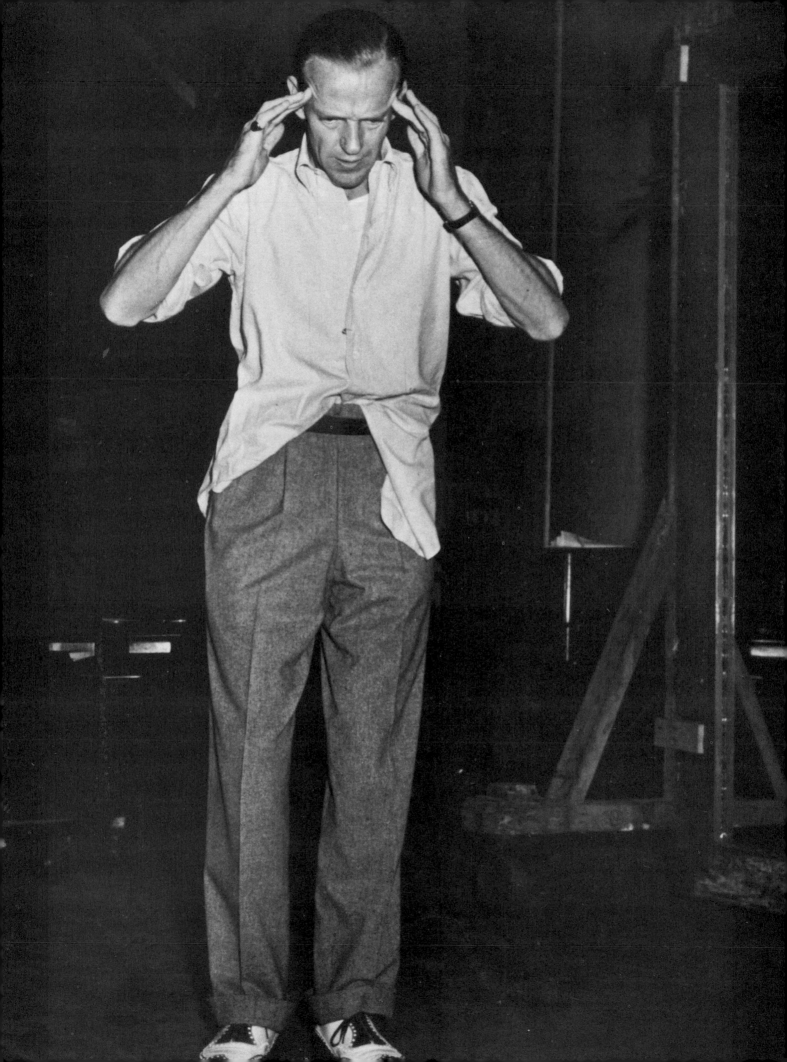

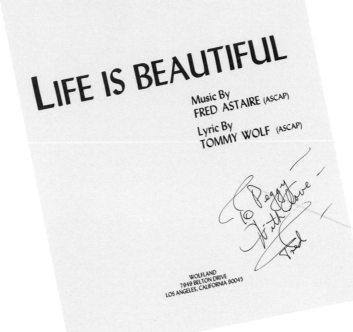

Sheet music of "Life Is Beautiful," dedicated to Peggy Self.

Fred is known, of course, as a dancer, but since all his stage and early film work was in the popular-musical form, he always had to sing as well. He never thought too much of his singing voice, but he soon became a model for other singers, and all the great contemporary composers of musical comedies delighted in writing songs for him. George Gershwin's last words were Fred's name, and his friend Noël Coward gave him the title for his autobiography, Steps in Time. *The composers who wrote songs for him included George and Ira Gershwin, Irving Berlin, Jerome Kern, Sigmund Romberg, Vincent Youmans, Howard Dietz and Arthur Schwartz, and Cole Porter. And to name just a few of the songs of theirs that Fred introduced: "Night and Day," "Lovely to Look At," "Begin the Beguine," "Flying Down to Rio," "Top Hat," "I Won't Dance," "A Fine Romance." Nobody ever had more songs written especially for him. Ironically, the major regret of his life was that he never wrote a hit song.*

As a singer, he was every songwriter's dream. Avoiding fancy interpretation of any kind, he developed a simple, direct style. He sang songs straight out, and his phrasing was the envy of every singer to come after him.

Practicing at home, 1959.

Fred Astaire, Gracie Allen, and George Burns.

Peter Duchin

I could be talking to you and sit and play, and it wouldn't change me at all. But Fred definitely changed the minute he started singing or talking about his dancing. He became a whole different person. I think he was very confident with his singing, though he never thought he was a very good singer. Fred was very musical—you could tell by the way he phrased. His sense of phrasing was most unusual for someone who was not a professional singer. By the end he *was* a professional singer, of course. When he sang "One for My Baby," he really phrased it extremely well. Sinatra phrases well, Vic Damone phrases well, but most people don't. Rhythm, of course, is obvious, but Fred also had a very good feeling for melody.

Stanley Donen

The person the great American composers—Gershwin, Berlin, Porter—liked most to have their songs sung by was Fred Astaire. He really was a true musician, who really did understand the music he worked with. They would all rather have Fred Astaire than anyone else. Just think of the songs he presented for the first time.

Carol Lynley

He wrote "Life Is Beautiful," which was sometimes used as a theme song for "The Tonight Show." There's also one song which he and Ava wrote together. And he wrote "City of the Angels" for Los Angeles.

Leslie Caron

He didn't think too much of his singing, but a lot of very professional singers think he was marvelous. I think he's absolutely wonderful, and of very pure pitch. He tackled singing with the attitude that you have to serve the song and the words and the story to be told. His singing was always witty, intelligent, and very charming.

Lady Alexandra Metcalfe

I had forgotten, until I saw the replay of all the films, how good a voice he had.

Anthony Perkins

I worked with Fred once, in *On the Beach,* and he was, for all his wonderful assurance when he put both feet down and moved, quite anxious about lines and dialogue. He was very unsure about accepting this role. Anyway, we spent a bit of time together in Australia. He must have been going through a period of time when he was feeling unsure of himself and somewhat frail, although he certainly did many things after that. *On the Beach* was a big production and there were long setups, so sometimes we had hours off. Fred and I used to drift off to the recording stage, where there was a huge grand piano, and I would sit down and play a little bit and he would sing the old Gershwin songs and the old Rodgers and Hart songs. I remember blessing my old piano teacher for being able to get me through a couple of choruses of "A Foggy Day," and to be able to transpose a little bit in order to find a key in which he'd be comfortable. That was great, lots of fun.

Betty Comden

I love the way he sings. He introduced more songs than anybody else.

Fred Astaire, Lewis Sobol, and Harry Belafonte.

Irving "Swifty" Lazar

He was the darling of the Ira Gershwins, the Jerome Kerns, and Cole Porter, and Irving Berlin, and Howard Dietz and Arthur Schwartz. Fred Astaire was a composer's dream. Ira Gershwin used to try songs out on him and me. He gave wonderful interpretations; that was as great a gift as his dancing. Gershwin was never interpreted better than by Fred Astaire. Irving Berlin thought he was the greatest that you can expect from a singer. I put Johnny Mercer in a movie—I think it was called *Daddy Long Legs*—at Twentieth, and that's how I met constantly with Fred. He was also a songwriter; he wrote very good songs.

Howard W. Koch

Fred wasn't a great singer, but he sure could sing a song. He made the song. He didn't have to sing like Sinatra; he just had that charisma.

Mrs. Oscar Levant

I met Fred in the late fifties, when Oscar had all his nervous breakdowns. He'd just come out of the sixth sanitarium, and was in the best shape he'd been in for years, but he hadn't performed in front of the public for a long time. Then he got a call to substitute for a talk-show host who was sick. He accepted, and he talked all about his hospitalization and his illness, and he was such an enormous hit that he was given a show of his own. Oscar got a telegram from Fred, and then a call, saying, "Can I come on your show?" It was a ninety-minute show, it was on twice a week, and no one got paid except Oscar. The only thing Fred said he didn't want to do was dance. Oscar adored Fred, absolutely adored him, and as a musician he knew that Astaire could sing a song better than anyone, and that every songwriter was thrilled to have Astaire sing their songs. Fred could sing better than Ezio Pinza, Oscar would say.

Roddy McDowall

I wish I'd seen him in the theater. It wasn't just his dancing. His singing was right up there with Ella Fitzgerald and Frank Sinatra. I'd rather hear Fred sing a song than almost anybody, because his phrasing was impeccable. He seemed to be the heartbeat, the pulse, of those composers. He understood it all. It was all main artery.

Ginger Rogers and Fred Astaire rehearsing *Carefree* with Irving Berlin, 1938.

Victor Young, Al Jolson, Fred Astaire, and George Jessel at the Hollywood Bowl Gershwin Concert, October 1937.

Rehearsing with Tommy Chambers for *You'll Never Get Rich*, 1941.

Fred Astaire with George and Ira Gershwin, rehearsing *Damsel in Distress*, 1937.

Audrey Hepburn

The way he expressed himself, not only through his dancing, but through his speaking, or his singing. He was such a good singer. Did I admire him as a singer? Oh yes. Oh God, yes. I mean, who didn't? I've no idea if he thought he was a good singer. Fred never thought he was good at anything. He was very self-effacing. You could always surmise, even from his pictures, that he was basically a very timid man who expressed himself through his dancing and his singing.

Liza Minnelli

I was asked to speak about him on "Nightline" the day he died, and as I listened to everyone else talk about his style, his elegance, his dancing, I suddenly thought about his contribution to pop music—popular music. He had more songs written for him than any other singer in history.

Ava Astaire

The one thing that really bothered him was that he didn't write a lot of hit songs. It was the one area of his life where he was not a total success, and it really bothered him. He enjoyed singing, and we used to sneak up to his door and listen to him playing the piano and singing. He did a lot of that alone—mainly his own songs. Songwriting was definitely his big gap.

Bill Self

He used to love to tinker on the piano and compose. I remember one of his songs, "Life Is Beautiful."

With Judy Garland in *Easter Parade*, 1948.

Limbering up at the piano before a studio rehearsal.

THE ACTOR

Kay Thompson, Fred Astaire, and
Audrey Hepburn in Paris, 1956.

In aviator costume, 1939.

He could also act, but just as he never considered himself much of a singer, he was very reluctant to think of himself as a serious actor. Yet everyone who watched him act, from John Gielgud to Anthony Perkins, found him flawless. In 1959, seventeen years before he stopped dancing, he played his first straight acting role, in On the Beach. He was in several more dramatic films, the last of which, Ghost Story, he made in 1981, five years before his death. If he had an acting rule, it was that he would not play ex-dancers or choreographers. Instead, he played a wide range of parts, including a scientist in On the Beach, a dog trainer in The Amazing Dobermans, and a con artist in The Towering Inferno, for which he was nominated for an Academy Award as best actor in a supporting role in 1974 (he lost out to Robert De Niro).

From 1958 to 1978, he was a popular actor in television, playing in such disparate programs as "Doctor Kildare" and "It Takes a Thief." In 1978 he won an Emmy for best actor in a dramatic role for his performance opposite Helen Hayes in A Family Upside Down. Although he never played on a soap opera, watching them was a favorite pastime for him.

Fred Astaire and Gordon Taylor in *Gay Divorce* at the Barrymore Theatre, November 1932.

Don Cook

One night Fred and Ava and Richard and Hermes Pan and I went to dinner at Patrone. It was the year Fred was nominated for best supporting actor for *The Towering Inferno*. Naturally, we all hoped he was going to win, and that he should win, and we were talking about this. I asked him if he was nervous about the awards, since he was obviously going to win. He answered, "No, I'm not! One of those boys from *The Godfather* is going to win." And he was right. It was Robert De Niro's first Oscar. I was stunned when they called out Robert De Niro and not Astaire.

Jack Haley, Jr.

When *That's Entertainment* was just about locked up, I got a call from Fred one day. He said, "Jack, I've got to see you. Can you come by the house on the way home?" I said I'd be by at around six-thirty. I was terrified he was going to ask for some drastic changes. Anyway, I get to the house and find the gate open. I whistle through, and he's standing in the doorway, looking very Fred Astaire. I go in and he takes me to the bar—he knows exactly what I drink, Smirnoff and Schweppes—and I can't figure out what's going on. Why is he making so sure that I have everything I could want? Anyway, we both have our drink, and he's being this charming and gracious host. Then he takes me on a minitour of the house, shows me his Cole Porter collage, and this and that. He doesn't sit, just stands behind his bar. I'm there at least an hour, rapping about how he studied under Bill "Bojangles" Robinson. Then I start to smell food cooking, and I know I'm not invited for dinner, and I've been there an hour, so finally I say, "Fred, is there something you wanted?" And he says, "Oh, I'm sorry, Jack, would you give me a few moments?" And he vanishes. I think, What the hell is going on? And he comes back wearing a Pierre Cardin raincoat, a beautiful new raincoat, and he says, "Remember the picture we talked about doing?" It was a movie called *On Borrowed Time,* at MGM, a fantasy originally with Lionel Barrymore, and we'd been talking about Fred and Jimmy Stewart doing it, with Jimmy playing the grandfather and Fred playing Death. Fred said that he thought that Death should be stylish. I agreed and assured him that he could wear the raincoat. He was so relieved.

Betty Comden

His acting was awfully good.

With Betty Compton in *Funny Face* at the Alvin Theatre, November 1927.

With Jesse Pearson and Ann-Margret on the set of *Bye Bye Birdie*, 1963.

Outside Buckingham Palace with Anne Heywood during the filming of *Midas Run*, June 1968.

Fred Astaire, Mel Ferrer, Audrey Hepburn, and the fashion model Dovima, during a break in the filming of *Funny Face*, 1956.

Tina Sinatra

I met Fred through Robert Wagner, about 1970. Fred was playing R.J.'s father on "It Takes a Thief." I played on it, too. And Bob and I were going together, so we'd socialize with Bob's friends, and one of them was Fred.

Leslie Caron

He had a great admiration for dramatic acting and straight actors. Once he said to me, "You and Crosby have been so smart to do straight acting. I wish I had done that." Of course, he went on to do it, but he wished he could have done really big parts. I thought his acting was very, very subtle. In one of his early films, he's in a plane and it crashes, and you see him coming down in flames, and he's so good! I mean, it's in the range of comedy, but he's a man about to die in an accident, and he's superbly subtle. Very good taste.

Scenarist Allan Scott and Fred Astaire during the filming of *Swing Time*, 1936.

George Murphy, Fred Astaire, and dance director Bobby Connelly during the filming of *Broadway Melody of 1940*, 1940.

Molly Keane

I remember one day I was speaking with John Gielgud. He was talking about Fred, and you know the way words just rush out of John's head and out of his mouth, without a thought of whether what he is saying about someone is good, bad, or indifferent. John said, "Oh, Fred is such a good actor. He could play *Hamlet.*" And that was before *On the Beach*.

Roddy McDowall

Ralph Richardson was in *The Midas Run,* the movie I made with Fred. Fred was in deep awe of Ralph, and it was lovely to watch Fred in such awe.

Carol Lynley

After he was seventy-six, he concentrated on his acting. He said, "I'm going to get this acting thing nailed down." And he kept up this interest in his career, really, until he was eighty-four, when he physically started to become too frail. He was going to do a project with Gene Kelly, but I think there was a problem of insurance. He was often on the phone to his agent, Michael Black.

Wardrobemen Eddie Polo and Maurice Brown soak Fred in preparation for a scene of *The Barkleys of Broadway*, 1949.

Michael Black

Fred would not dance anymore by the time I met him. He would never even play a role where he was a retired dancer or a choreographer. Certain roles he just didn't want to do—an older person of any kind. He realized that the type of roles which he would do would not be plentiful. He still enjoyed the notion, though, if the situation was right. The project we were proudest of was *A Family Upside Down,* for which he won an Emmy for best actor. He loved Helen Hayes. He wanted to be acknowledged as an actor.

Anthony Perkins

What was he best at as an actor? Standing still. He had a beautiful stillness, an authenticity, a simplicity; just a little shift of his head in any of his acting scenes would be very eloquent. He was very austere. He wasn't all over the place. Did he rehearse a lot for his acting scenes? No. Dance sequences he felt he owned, and he felt responsible for those; they were his creations and his right. But as an actor of dialogue, it was almost as if he wasn't really there. He had a wonderful diffidence, a wonderful lack of taking himself seriously. When he acted, in *On the Beach,* for instance, he didn't want people watching, and that was nice.

His only passionate screen kiss, with Lilli Palmer in *The Pleasure of His Company,* March 1960.

HIS FAME AND MODESTY

Fred Astaire was as shy and self-effacing as he was famous and unmistakable. He didn't like people making a fuss over him, and he was embarrassed whenever he was faced with any form of public adulation. However, there was no way he could avoid making an incredible impact wherever he went. Perhaps that's why he usually wore sunglasses in his walks around Beverly Hills, and why he always chose to dine in restaurants that he knew well, where he could be sure of being seated discreetly.

Reticent though he was about his own fame, he was an avid fan of other performers he admired. He often asked friends whether they thought they could arrange for him to meet this or that film or television star; it never occurred to him that any one of them would have died to meet him.

David Bailey's portrait of Fred Astaire taken in Ireland, 1978.

With autograph hunters.

Ava Astaire

Daddy never understood why people recognized him, he really didn't. He was always so surprised, on one hand, and on the other hand he took it as his due.

Richard McKenzie

I had a gallery in Los Angeles, so I knew quite a lot of the celebrities around town. Fred would often ask if I knew so and so, and could we have them to dinner, since he'd like to meet them. What he didn't realize was that, even if I didn't know them, anyone would have accepted. He loved the game shows on television, and he loved meeting the stars of those shows.

Gene Rayburn

Fred and I were very close friends. We never worked together. We had a mutual-admiration society going. I met him because he wanted to meet me, and a mutual friend threw a party, and we were friends ever after. I was thrilled to meet him and his sister. They were both marvelous people. Gentle people.

Lady Alexandra Metcalfe

He was a sweet, sweet man, and very, very humble. One was never aware that he even thought of himself as a star. I'm talking about the early twenties, when I met him.

Twiggy

I went to Los Angeles in 1971 to promote *The Boy Friend,* which was done by MGM, and somebody in the publicity department asked me if there were any stars I would like to meet. I thought, What a weird question—it was so Hollywood—but I said, "There is one I would really love to meet, and that's Fred Astaire." Everybody went quiet, and they said, "Well, he's a very private man, and he doesn't really see people. Is there anyone else?" So I said, "Not really. And I certainly wouldn't want to intrude on his privacy. I understand that." And then I forgot about it. The next day I got a phone call from the MGM offices to say that one of the secretaries had overheard all this, and she'd been with MGM for many years and knew Fred Astaire personally. When I had left the studio, she had rung him at home and told him what happened. Through her he'd extended an invitation to me to come up to his house for tea. Well, I was very nervous. Ava told me a few years later that her father had asked her to stick around that day because he'd invited Twiggy to tea and he was very nervous, which is so sweet. We had a wonderful tea. He was a lovely man, very modest. Every time I did anything after that, I always got a little note from him.

Tina Sinatra

Every year, for eighteen years, I called him on May 10. But he hated to have a fuss made over his birthday.

Stanley Donen

When I was twenty-six, I directed Fred Astaire. Fred Astaire was a gigantic monument in my life. I twice tried to tell him that, and he just didn't want to know. He didn't want to hear it, he didn't want to respond to it. He didn't want the responsibility of being that.

Hermes Pan

He never liked to talk about his past, and he would become irritated when people asked him about when he did this and when he did that. He would say, "I've done it, and that's that. Now I want to talk about what I'm *going* to do." I remember one night some lady was here, and she was talking about things that were really annoying Fred. She was saying why didn't he do this and why didn't he do that, and suddenly he said, "Madam, I don't give a damn about what you think."

Katharine Hepburn

I don't think he was vain at all, I think he was just brilliant. Not at all vain, and an absolute perfectionist, which is always nice.

Ava Astaire

Travel was so difficult, with the fans bothering him and all that. The last time I traveled with him was in the early seventies, when Richard and I came over here to Ireland. He came over at the same time to make a record with Bing Crosby. On our flight from London, there were two seats on each side that faced the whole rest of the plane, and those were the seats we got. He wouldn't complain. He wouldn't make a fuss to have them change it. He just didn't want to cause even more attention to be brought to himself.

Leonard Gershe

He never asked me if I saw such and such a movie. It was a job. He was truly modest, as opposed to Gene, who thinks he's hot stuff, and he is, but he knows it. Fred had no awareness of how good he really was, or why it seemed exceptional to anybody else. He didn't just get out there and flow. He worked hard, but it was innate, inherent.

Stanley Donen

The only time I ever heard him being remotely pleased with himself was at the American Film Institute awards in 1981. They'd shown clips of him dancing with Ginger, Audrey, and others, and Fred got up and said, "It wasn't too bad, was it?"

Hermes Pan

He knew he was good. He would say, "Yes, I dance, and yes, I do it well."

Leslie Caron

He was intelligent, and I think the ones who get carried away with their fame are not the greatest thinkers. Fred was of the period when your duty, if you were to be paid, was to entertain. You were not allowed to bore people, to give them something slapdash.

Bill Self

One day Fred rang me and asked me if I could get a CBS tape for his friend Jock Whitney. Well, Jock Whitney was Bill Paley's brother-in-law, but it was interesting to me that Fred didn't quite think that his name or Jock Whitney's name would do the trick. Fred was always unassuming. It was not an act. He was aware that he was Fred Astaire, that people stared at him and wanted his autograph, but it never went to his head.

Sam Goldwyn, Jr.

I was very impressed with that little piece he did on *That's Entertainment,* when he talked about movies and said, "Well, we never really thought about it. We just went to work on Monday." You realized that he had created this incredible body of work, unlike anybody else's. He had such humility about it. I remember when we did those three TV specials and he said to me, "It was kind of exciting, because it's all new, but you never quite get those things right." He was always very critical of what he did.

Anne Slater

I met Fred with Bing Crosby. I was in Bing's car, driving into Paramount, and Fred was walking toward it. He recognized the car, because the driver gave a little toot to warn him to step out of the way. He did thirty seconds of twists and twirls and then rushed around the car, opened the door, and saw me. He'd never seen me before in his life, and he was mortified—so embarrassed. "Oh, please forgive me." Well, I was thrilled. I'd had my own little private show.

Mrs. Oscar Levant

After the shooting of *Daddy Long Legs,* Fred went to Paris. He found a secluded hotel so that nobody would know he was there. Then he wanted the company of a young lady, so he asked the concierge where there was a small, respectable place he could go and remain unknown. The concierge suggested somewhere anonymous, and when Fred rang the bell and the door was opened, the woman in charge exclaimed, *"O! Papa Long Legs!"*

Don Cook

I had a small dinner party when Ava and Richard were in town. I asked Sammy Davis and Altovise and Eddie Peterson, who works for Sammy. Then I thought, Why don't we call Elizabeth Taylor and see if she's doing anything? So there we are at the table, and all of a sudden in comes Elizabeth. Ava was thrilled, and when she told her father about it the next day, he said, "Damn! Why didn't you ask me to go? I would have gone like a shot." He was a big fan of Taylor's.

Ava Astaire

When *Liberty* magazine was revived in the seventies, they wanted to pay a tribute to him as being the entertainer of the century, and he got really quite annoyed because he hated having to have tributes. He said to Richard and me, "You know, this is going to be a terrible nuisance, but I'm going to do it because if I don't they'll give it to someone else, and that would be wrong."

Audrey Hepburn

I said in a nutshell what I thought of Fred Astaire at the American Film Institute award ceremony in 1981. I walked up and down the room for three weeks writing that one half a minute they give you to say something in. I mean, how do you draw the picture of somebody in a few words? Well, if I may say so myself, I did a good job, because it is the way I feel about him, in that sense. It's maybe not sufficient compared to what other people feel. I don't know if you've ever been to one of those evenings, but this was the best—and everyone says it was the best—because they showed a lot of clips, and so you saw all those marvelous musical numbers one after the other. It was so entertaining, and David Niven was the master of ceremonies, and all the people who'd worked with Fred who were still around were there.

I said, "One look at this most debonair and elegant and distinguished of legends, and I could feel myself turn into solid lead while my heart sank into my two left feet. Then suddenly I felt a hand around my waist, and with his inimitable grace and lightness Fred literally swept me off my feet."

Selling war bonds to his delighted
fans.

THE ASTAIRE WOMEN

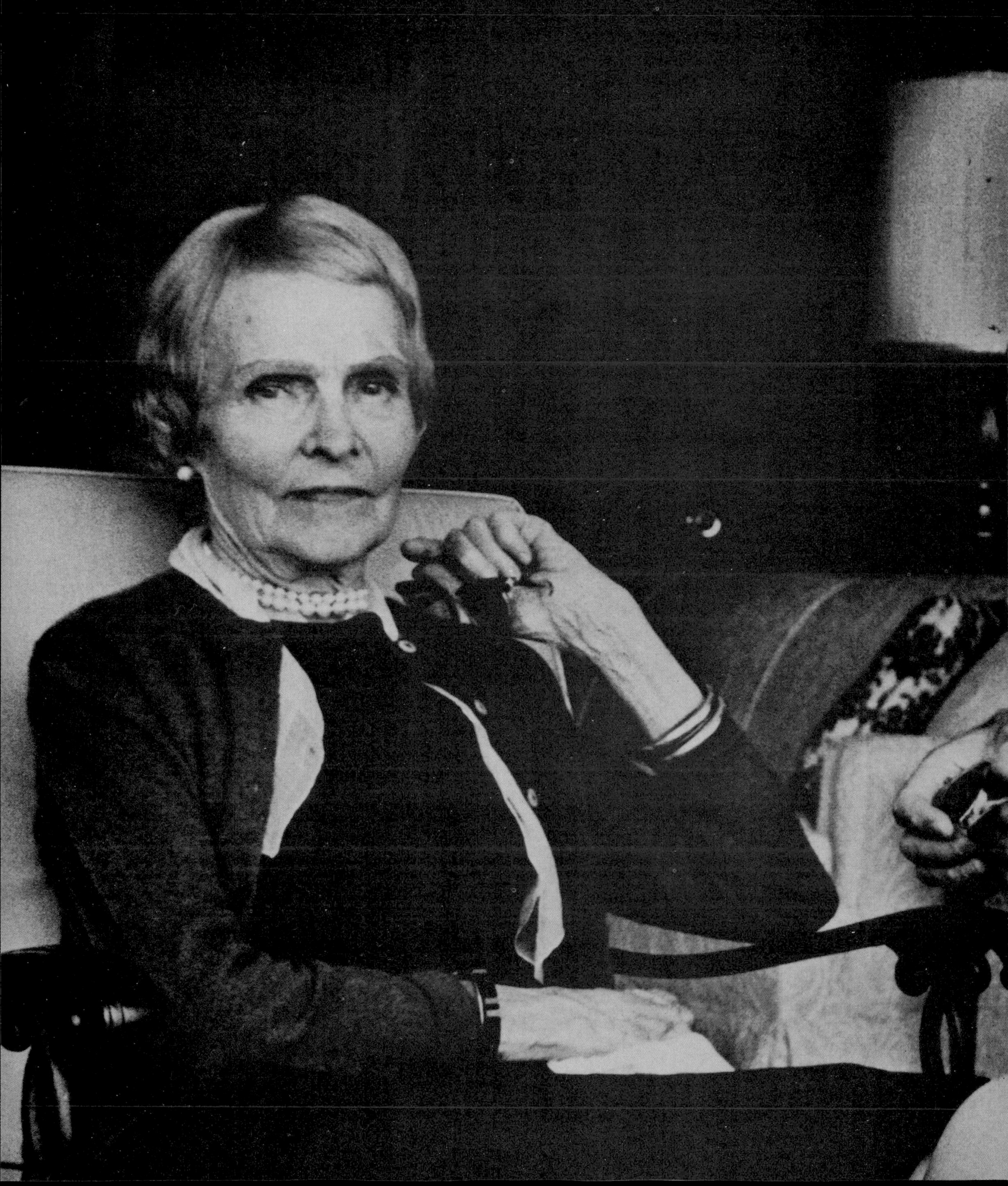

Passport photo taken for Ann's first Atlantic crossing to England, March 1923.

December 1926.

red was born Frederick Austerlitz on May 10, 1899, in Omaha, Nebraska. His father, also Frederick Austerlitz, was born in Vienna and came to America in 1895. Fred's mother, Ann Geilus, was of Alsatian origin. Fred and his sister, Adele, showed such talent as small children that when Fred was four and a half his mother took them to New York to launch them in a theatrical career. Fred's father, whose idea it was to adopt the stage name Astaire for them, stayed in Omaha. For the rest of Fred's life, Ann continued to be a mainstay. She pushed him and his sister through dance school, into vaudeville, and later onto the Broadway stage. She also went to England with them when they were invited to appear on the London stage. After Fred and Adele broke up as a team and both married, Ann Astaire divided her time between their two households. She was living in Hollywood with Fred when she died in 1975, at the age of ninety-six.

Ann and her son, 1959.

Ann and Fred at Santa Anita Racetrack, 1940.

Ann visiting Fred on the set of *Roberta*, 1935.

Ann and Fred, March 1935.

Hermes Pan

Fred's mother was a very lovely lady. Fred took wonderful care of her until she died. She had her room in his house, and she was always treated like a queen. She would call him Sonny.

Molly Keane

Mrs. Astaire talked to me about Fred's serious influence on Dellie, making her practice the routines with him, even when he was a boy. Later, when Dellie was the one who was sparkling and captivating the world, it was Fred's discipline that controlled her. Then she was the brilliant one that all the critics went absolutely mad about. And Fred was the supporter, the lesser partner, more or less in the background. Dellie and Fred were absolutely part of each other. He was the influence on Dellie's life, and in a way on his mother's. She was a remarkable woman. Beautiful, absolutely beautiful. Lord Charles Cavendish, Dellie's husband, simply adored her. He used to call her Mother Ann. Mrs. Astaire told me once that when she was producing Fred and Adele as children, you know, in the days when she took them round to all this dancing stuff, one evening there was exactly one egg left for supper. She scrambled it and divided it between two bits of toast and gave them each a piece. She told this story to Charlie, Dellie's husband, and me at Lismore one day, and Charlie sort of shook his head and said, "I bet Mother Ann didn't eat a thing that night." And she laughed as if she were remembering the happiest day of her life.

Anne Slater

Adele and Fred's mother was the most superb woman. She mended every single one of the many tapestries that hang in the library at Lismore. She was there all during the war, with Adele and Charlie, and those tapestries were in shreds. Both Ann and Dellie were marvelous needle women.

Molly Keane

Fred had a lot of his mother's look, and she really was a lean beauty. Sometimes I felt he was more like a father than a son, to her and Dellie both. Charlie was Mrs. Astaire's naughty son. When he was dying, she was his great friend and support. She was marvelous to him.

On a transatlantic liner, 1932.

Leslie Caron

I was married to someone who was a great admirer of Fred, so when *Daddy Long Legs* was finished, I called him up and we went to see him. After we'd been there fifteen minutes, he said, "I must introduce you to my mother." He was seventy-two! Well, she couldn't have been more jaunty. She had lovely ankles, a lovely waist, bright eyes, and a wonderfully fresh complexion. She was terribly sweet, and she said, "Oh, you're the little girl who danced with my Fred."

Tina Sinatra

He talked a lot about the past with me. I knew his mother very well. She didn't die long before he did. I used to go and visit her at his house. He'd be at the drums, this delicate thing, and she was a little bird. She'd send me poetry, and I'd send her cards and flowers on her birthday.

Stanley Donen

One night in 1978, I went up to Fred's house to collect him to go out to dinner, and he said, "Hang on. I'm just going to kiss my mother good-night." Fred was seventy-nine then.

Richard McKenzie

Fred was staying at the Connaught during one London visit, and he hated the Connaught. One morning I came down and found him sitting all alone near the door, so I sat down with him so that he wouldn't be accosted. A very flamboyant older man came to the desk, and he was asking for Fred Astaire's room number. He said, "All I want to do is leave him a note." He was covered in jewelry. He passed us then and recognized Fred, and didn't know what to do about it. The man said to us, "Don't worry. I'm very well off. I'm not going to touch you for anything." Then he said, "Your mother was very kind to me once, and I just wanted to tell you so in a note." So Fred said, "Come and sit down." The man had been a chorus boy when they were touring, and he had taken them to see the sights. Ann had picked him out because she thought he looked the most cultured. Fred was thrilled with this, and we all three had tea together.

During the making of *The Barkleys of Broadway*, 1949.

Fred Junior, Ann, Fred, Ava, and Peter, 1958.

HIS SISTER, ADELE

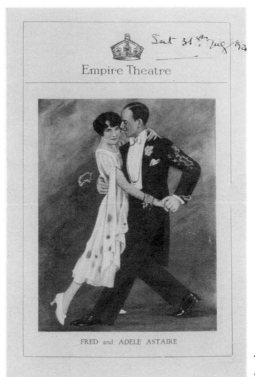

FRED and ADELE ASTAIRE

The program for *Lady, Be Good!* at the Empire Theatre, London, 1926.

Adele Astaire was born September 10, 1897, two years before Fred. She and her younger brother entered vaudeville as a children's act in 1905. Their first Broadway show was Over the Top in 1917, and they were the rage of the musical theater, both in America and England, in such shows as Lady, Be Good!, Funny Face, Gay Divorcee, and The Band Wagon, until 1932, when Dellie retired from show business to marry Lord Charles Cavendish, the Duke of Devonshire's younger brother. Adele and Charlie lived at Lismore Castle, the Cavendish family seat in Ireland. All three of their children, a daughter and twin sons, died a few hours after birth. Charlie Cavendish died of drink in 1944, at the age of thirty-nine. In 1947 Adele married Kingman Douglass, an investment banker. They had homes in New York and Jamaica until 1971, when they retired to Phoenix, Arizona. Douglass died there two years later. Adele, a popular socialite all her life, continued to divide her time between Phoenix and Lismore Castle until she died of a stroke in 1981. She and Fred, whom she loved to tease, were on the most intimate terms all her life.

Adele, aged twenty-one, and Fred, aged nineteen, in 1919.

Adele and Fred about 1910.

Fred and Adele in 1905.

Mrs. Jock Whitney
My husband and Fred Astaire became friends when Jock was at Oxford and Fred and his sister, Adele, were appearing in *Lady, Be Good!* in London. On the closing night of the show the Prince of Wales gave a party at St. James's Palace in honor of Fred and Adele, and Fred asked if he could include Jock. At an early-morning hour, Fred had confided to His Royal Highness that the American at Oxford was an expert dancer and might give a demonstration of the latest dance craze in the United States, the Black Bottom. All the gold chairs surrounding the dance floor were pushed back, and Jock had nowhere to go except to make a try at the Black Bottom. He did a few steps and then fell flat on his own bottom.

Sam Goldwyn, Jr.
It was strange getting to know Adele after knowing Fred. They went to work pretty young, and they were stars. And they worked constantly. Adele told me that Fred loved it and she didn't. She just genuinely didn't care for it. That happens to stage people—either they want to break with it or they stay with it. Adele talked like a sailor. She was married to Lord Charles Cavendish, who died of drink. I stayed with her at Lismore after Charlie died, and I remember sitting there with her one day. I was looking at her, and she said, "I know what you're thinking. How different I am from Fred." She had a wicked sense of humor. When she got mad at someone, she would write their name on a piece of paper and put it in her shoe.

The Duke of Devonshire
Adele was really most tremendous fun. She was very coarse, and for that reason everyone thought, when she married Uncle Charlie, that she and my grandmother would be a disaster; but she and my grandmother hit it off very well. She was very, very funny, really awfully funny. She was an astonishingly good woman, because there was Charlie, a hopeless alcoholic, and she put up with it. The other really wonderful woman was Adele's mother. She kept that estate going. She was a great, great woman. As you get older, your idiosyncrasies get worse, and, without being prudish, Adele did get astonishingly coarse. She remarried around 1947, and in the sixties she came back to Lismore, and Fred used to come over and stay. I owed a very great deal to Adele and Charlie, because they left me Lismore. Not only did I love the place, but it was in my interest as heir apparent to go and spend time there.

Sir Robert Throckmorton

I met Fred and Adele before the war, in about 1931, when they were in *The Band Wagon* on Broadway. I would also see him in those days in London. I used to go and have supper with them after the show, and with their mother also. I continued to see Adele a lot, because her husband, Charlie Cavendish, was a great friend of mine.

Patricia Prior

I was Adele's companion and secretary. I first saw Fred Astaire when I was a child in Lismore—my mother comes from Lismore. It was after Lord Charles's death, when Adele used to come to Lismore with her mother and her brother, and I used to visit my grandparents in the summers in Lismore. But I didn't meet Mr. Astaire properly until I was living with Adele in America. She lived in the Dorchester, on Fifty-seventh Street, in New York. I have never, ever, seen any brother and sister so close. It was phenomenal. They laughed, they joked, they talked for hours. Adele would get on the telephone to Los Angeles, and that telephone bill must have been just outrageous. I would say, "Don't you realize this is a long-distance call?" and she would say, "But this is my brother, my baby brother." They were absolute opposites. She was a character, very outgoing but rather shy. Her outgoingness covered up the shyness. She didn't care what she said. But he was so quiet and reserved. When she would come out with something outrageous, he would just say, "That's my sister." It never really bothered him. I never heard him say anything against her, never, ever, because that was her. She put a few people down from time to time, but she did it in such a way that she got away with it. Adele moved to Arizona in February of 1971, and I went, too. Mr. Douglas, Adele's second husband, died soon after their move, so she stayed in Arizona so that she could be close to her mother and her brother. They really were very close to their mother. They'd visit each other, back and forth. They would play golf together and go for long walks. Fred and Adele spent her last Christmas together. He came to Phoenix, even though it was the first Christmas he was married to Robyn, to spend it with her, just months before she died. Before, Fred always said, "Oh, Christmas bothers me. I don't like it." But this last Christmas they insisted on spending together. Then Fred went straight back to Hollywood, and my family and Adele spent New Year's Eve together. At midnight, Michael Jackson called to wish Adele a happy new year. And then Fred called her after that. He called one minute after midnight.

During *Lady, Be Good!* at the Liberty Theatre, New York, December 1924.

Adele Astaire, December 1928.

Bill Self
Adele was very salty, and she loved to reminisce about the past.

Slim Keith
My then husband, Leland Hayward, was a very young man, and he was making his way, kind of, in movies. It was the first agenting he ever did. He had seen, of an evening, Fred and Adele Astaire in a musical in which they did a couple of turns together. I can't remember what it was called. He went backstage after the show and said, "My name is Leland Hayward, and I can double the money you make every night." They asked how, and he said, "You just do your routines, stay in costume, and I'll have a car outside the theater which will take you to a nightclub, and there you'll simply do the dance which you have just done. Very soon, I'll get you a night what you get a week." And so Leland became Fred's agent. And he remained Fred's agent for many years.

Radie Harris
Fred first came into my life when he and Adele were doing *Lady, Be Good!* and all those early musicals. I remember Fred telling me that he was always the first one in the theater, and Dellie was the last one out. He always came in and practiced before the show, and Dellie would arrive at just about curtain rise. They couldn't have been more opposite, but he adored her, and she adored him.

Jeanne Vanderbilt
I didn't know Dellie, and I was dying to meet her. Finally Phyllis said to me, "We can't do that. Fred won't have it, because of Dellie's language."

Molly Keane
It must have been during the war or just afterwards that Dellie made a film, or did tests for a film. I saw some of the stills, but you know you can't tell anything from stills. Fred said it was a no-good picture and stopped her doing it. He didn't want her lessened in any way. He just wouldn't let her do it. I forget who it was who was doing the film, but it was some quite big affair. Fred just washed it out and said, "You can't do it." Dellie was totally unafraid of anything or anybody, totally without any kind of embarrassment. Sometimes she used to get terribly exhausted and bored because she gave so much of herself. She was there all the time, and there'd be no rest, from even her best friends.

**A gouache of Adele
by Cecil Beaton.**

Passport photo, 1927.

Jean Howard

Adele was completely outgoing, completely with it, great fun at a party—drank, had a hell of a good time. Fred was completely opposite. She was just a darling, a lot of fun. I met her in New York when I lived there. Brother and sister adored each other.

Slim Keith

Adele was more like Bea Lillie. She was a clown, funny, marvelous to talk to. She was very lively, much more so than Fred.

Lady Alexandra Metcalfe

I have no memory of being mesmerized by Dellie, though she was very, very bubbly. She used the most ghastly four-letter words in conversation, which Fred never did.

Eleanor Lambert

I met Fred with Adele in Los Angeles. I went to his house with her. Adele was wonderful. She was just as outgoing as Fred was ingoing. She was also extremely short-tempered. He avoided trouble, and she made it.

Carol Lynley

Dellie was an extraordinary woman, very tiny and very elegant, and she had the most obscene mouth of any woman I ever knew. Even I couldn't tell you the things she used to say. Dellie was outrageous, and it all came out of this very upper-crust, well-dressed person. Sometimes I would go out to a restaurant in Beverly Hills with her and Fred and Hermes, and Dellie would break into songs that they had done in vaudeville, and Fred would join in sometimes. Of the two, she was the leader.

Leonard Gershe

Dellie loved to upset him. I remember being at the Bistro. Dellie and Gloria Romanoff and Frances Goldwyn were there. Dellie was telling us about a pillow she was working on for the guest room, and she said, "It's wonderful. It says WELCOME on the front, and then on the back it says FUCK OFF." Fred's face fell, and he said imploringly, "Dellie." He cringed and went red. Dellie shrieked, "They've heard it before, Fred, don't worry." She had twinkle. She twinkled all over. If she walked into a room you could see her star quality immediately.

Aileen Mehle (Suzy)

The first time I really met Fred and sat next to him was at a party in the town house of Trumbull Barton in New York. I think it was a dinner party for Fred and Adele, about twenty years ago. When we descended the staircase, and were all saying good-night to one another, Adele reached over exuberantly to kiss Fred good night on the cheek, and he said, "Watch the rug." Adele had all the zip the world ever set out. They were wonderful together. She adored him, and he adored her. It was, all their lives, the closest of friendships. He would roll his eyes back in his head sometimes, but of course who wouldn't who knew Dellie? There was no way there wouldn't be fun when she was around. Instant dynamite.

Dominick Dunne

The first time I met the famous Adele Astaire was at Ava's first wedding. She was every bit as outspoken and outrageous as all the stories I'd heard made her out to be. You didn't have to know her for two years before she would get like that either. It was hello, hello, and boom, out it came.

Hermes Pan

Adele would kid Fred and call him Moaning Minnie, because she said nothing ever pleased him.

Molly Keane

Dellie used to scream with laughter over dirty books. She would cry out, "Oh, my dear, this is filthy." I remember a wonderful thing that Dellie once said. I hadn't been writing for quite a long time, and Dellie always said I ought to go on, and this time she said, "Why don't you write a book about some of those Irish ladies—you know, those terrible old sisters who live together and who are always sticking knitting needles into the canary's eyes." I finally wrote something after a long time, and the publishers had a party for me in Dublin. When I arrived home, there was a pile of letters for me on the table. One was from Dellie's lawyer, to say she'd left me a thousand pounds.

Leslie Caron

His sister was a really swinging old lady. I remember meeting her in Jamaica, where she had a house. She was so elegant. She had the latest Gucci. She was about seventy-eight, and jogged every morning. She and Fred both had this unbelievable health. Of course, they were Austrian.

Aboard the *Majestic* on their way to England to star in *Lady, Be Good!*, January 1926.

Anne Slater

I met Adele in Jamaica. She had a house at Roundhill. She was very cute and funny, and very naughty, very of the twenties. She wore her hair in a little bob—sort of Louise Brooks. It was very hard to make her sit down and behave. Fred and Adele were the closest brother and sister I've ever known.

Douglas Fairbanks, Jr.

Fred was devastated by Dellie's death. He and I were filming *Ghost Story* in Saratoga when the news came. Robyn, his second wife, to whom he had just got married, was unable to be with him. He asked me to move into the hotel bedroom which adjoined his so that we could leave the door open at night. Such was his sadness that he didn't want to be alone.

Molly Keane

Fred and Dellie never seemed to be out of touch. When he was back in America, a parcel would suddenly arrive—a record or a new song that Fred had sent. Dellie was mad about every table game, from canasta to Scrabble, and Fred used to send any new ones over to her.

Horst P. Horst's portrait of Adele playing canasta.

Reading *The Tatler* in London, 1926.

A theatrical benefit performance to raise money for the Vineyard Shore Workers School, in the 1920s.

Dear Dellie:

Was delighted with your letter—and listen cutie—I know how you "slay 'em" over there—but it doesn't surprise me babe, you always have!! You seem to think it's unusual or something—listen kid you are terrific!!

"Little Dellie" thinks I've forgotten all about her—no fear babe—I know everything—I get loads of English clippings about you and they are swell!

I think your Cecil Beaton picture is beautiful—and I've just sent it to Margaret Case of *Vogue*—she wired me for it. She promised to send it right back.

Glad you liked *Roberta*—it is dynamite in the box-office here in this country and I think it will be in London too.

It stayed five weeks in Boston in a theatre that rarely holds anything for even two weeks.

It has been held over everywhere—and many places for three, four and five weeks!

Isn't it nice! You didn't say how you liked the dances. They're all new you know babe!

I've got all new ones in *Top Hat* too—about five of 'em.

So far so good with this one—it looks alright and the numbers are swell. It's a goofy comedy plot and seems to be working out well—at least several things that I know you'll like. The next picture they're planning for me towards the end of the year—I'm a sailor!!!! . . .

George is with me now and is perfectly wonderful. He does everything. Serves table when I want him to—drives car—typewrites correspondence—and I even used him in one scene in this picture. He is thrilled beyond words. His quota number and passport etc. are all fine so he can stay permanently.

A lot of stars have press agents as you say in your letter—Bennett and G. Rogers I think too and many others—but I wouldn't have one as a gift. I have all I can do to keep the press department from bothering the life out of me at the studio. I refuse everything they ask me to do and still a lot of sappy stuff gets out—but it doesn't mean anything to those mugs that read the movie mags—however don't show this to anybody because if a mag got hold of it they'd love to print what I think!!!! Mother was swell here—do take good care of her—babe. . . .

Hope Charlie will not overdo the drinking thing—it's so wrong if his health suffers by it. I'm all for him getting a bit squiffed now and then but if it hurts the health!!! No!!

I'm bothered to hell by a fan club in my name. Some girl in Jersey City has got it going and they print a paper etc. and I have to write and wire every now and then and it's all such a lot of balls but I have to do it. They hold tremendous theatre parties and go in a mass when my pictures come there and they have pictures taken outside the theatre etc.

They want you to be an honorary member, so when they write—just answer and say, "thanks—of course I would" etc., etc., something nice. I get many other requests from people who want to start other clubs in my name but I say "No" because one is plenty. My fan mail totals about 17,000 letters a month which is supposed to be terrific—especially for me in pictures so short a time and doing few pictures. Fan mail gives me a pain in the neck. It's such a lot of balls—everybody wants to learn to dance etc., etc. I am publishing a book as soon as I can get time to edit it—there will unquestionably be a big sale for it if we get a good interesting and instructive set-up. They're calling me to the set—so I must run—it's lots of fun here— all the boys are swell—so much more amusing than the lousy stage. I hope I don't ever have to do stage again— except possibly a personal appearance tour for a few weeks.

Have already had an offer of $15,000 a week with Rogers—but I don't want to do any now—I haven't time and I would only consider it alone anyway—I know I can get $10,000 alone.

Thursday May 8th.

Well—I guess I'll get this off sweetie—I only have one shot this morning—the rest of the day I'll spend rehearsing "Cheek to Cheek," a swell tune—sort of different. It's a cross between "The Last Round-up" and "Night and Day," has no verse and the chorus runs something like seventy-two bars!! Figure that out. . . .

If you are in London when Ed Everett Horton is I told him to call you up. He leaves here in June and is the nicest person—so be sweet to him. He is in this picture and is so swell. I believe old Ed is a little bit of a pansy . . . doesn't quite know himself—however—do not camp with him—he is apt not to understand—I mean do not poke anything at him!!

You'll adore him.

Am sorry you were not there for Sam and Frances Goldwyn—they are so grand and we spend much time with them. She is swell and Sam is really a peach and funny!

Jimmy Cagney came over and watched me shoot part of my "Top Hat" number—he is a great guy! Sends me fan wires on each picture. Wish I could write more now—be good sweetie and take care of Ma—also Charlie—and yourself—no fancy autodriving by Chas. coming home from one of those Irish sprees at night.

Best love babe—

Phyllis is fine and sends love. . . .

In *The Band Wagon* at the New Amsterdam Theatre, New York, June 1931.

Mrs. Kingman Douglass (Adele) and
her brother, 1959.

Phyllis and Fred Astaire with Lord
and Lady Charles Cavendish at
Lismore Castle, Ireland, in the 1940s.

Fred and Adele in Holywood.

Fred Astaire, Letter to Adele, July 18, 1937

Dellie Darling:

Wasn't it sad about poor Georgie Gershwin? He had a rotten time, out of his mind the last few days. That brain tumor struck suddenly and viciously. He could not talk or do anything. I did not see him—it was too late—nobody was allowed to see him the last few days. Ira told me the last word he spoke was my name. In trying to make himself understood it came out and then he collapsed and never was able to function again. It's all so cruel—poor George. His body was sent to N.Y. and they had a big funeral there and here they held memorial services in his honour. I sent flowers for you and mother. Poor Ira—he is so crushed, as you know they were never apart. It is difficult for me to work with all of the songs in the new picture without constantly thinking of George. He did a very good score for us—I think better than *Shall We Dance*. . . .

Letter from Fred to Dellie, written when George Gershwin died.

Photograph of Fred and Adele by Cecil Beaton.

Peter Potter with Phyllis, Fred Junior in arms, and Fred.

HIS FIRST WIFE, PHYLLIS

Fred Astaire and Phyllis Livingstone Potter on their wedding day, July 12, 1933.

 red Astaire's first wife, and the mother of his children, was born Phyllis Baker in 1904. Her mother deserted her when she was a child, and after her father, a respected Boston doctor, remarried, Phyllis was brought up by her aunt and uncle, Mr. and Mrs. Henry Bull. Her uncle was a New York social figure, head of the Turf and Field Club. In 1927 Phyllis married Eliphalet Nott Potter III, and they had one son, Peter. She got divorced from Potter in 1932. Fred and Phyllis were married on July 12, 1933, when Phyllis was twenty-five and Fred was thirty-three. They moved immediately to California, where Fred entered pictures, and they soon became one of the leading couples of the Old Hollywood. Fred junior was born in 1936, and Ava, in 1942. After twenty-one years of blissful marriage, Phyllis died of lung cancer in 1954.

Phyllis and Ava Astaire.

Sam Goldwyn, Jr.

I've known Fred since the time I was a little boy. The Astaires and my parents used to dine at least once a week. My mother and Phyllis were very close friends, along with Mrs. Berlin. They were all three sort of outsiders in this community. Phyllis was a little tiny woman. She'd been married before, and had a child, Peter Potter, and we used to play together as children, since we were the same age.

Lily Guest

I was a great friend of Phyllis's. We went to school together. When I went out to California, she could not have been nicer to me. I went out and stayed with Liz Whitney, after I got my divorce, and Phyllis used to come and pick me up every day. I would spend all day with her. I think she enjoyed old friends coming to visit.

Sir Robert Throckmorton

I knew Phyllis very well. I was a friend of her aunt and uncle, Mr. and Mrs. Bull, who brought her up. She didn't really like what one imagined Hollywood to be. She and Fred both liked a nice quiet life. They were busy building their house when I was there. I really think that Phyllis would have preferred to live somewhere else. She built a little house next door to theirs for her aunt and uncle, so that they could come and visit her whenever possible.

Hermes Pan

Phyllis was a lovely lady. She just didn't understand Hollywood informality: She was a New York socialite. She scared the life out of most of the people in Hollywood. All the producers felt ill at ease around her, because she was a little too formal for them. She had a lisp and a funny *r*, so Fred would imitate her saying there was a perfectly *dweadful* man at the door, and it was David Niven, whom she didn't know yet, dropping by after tennis. Later, David Niven was a good friend of hers. Joan Crawford was a good friend of Phyllis's. So were Merle Oberon and Sylvia Ashley and Gable and Cole Porter.

  She was very proper. She never came on the set, and if she did she would only stay a few minutes. I could count the times that she came to the set. She was a very good friend of mine, and in her social manner she was very down to earth. When I built this house, she helped me design it. She painted that fireplace; she said it was a perfectly dweadful fireplace and that it had to be painted black. She came up here in Levi's with a paintbrush and painted the inside of the fireplace for me. She loved to go to the ranch they had. She loved to get out and work with the horses and in the garden.

Mr. and Mrs. Fred Astaire on their honeymoon, October 1933.

Phyllis and Fred on board a liner.

Opposite: Phyllis Astaire dressed as Elissa Landi in *Warrior's Husband* and Fred Astaire as Maurice Chevalier in *The Smiling Lieutenant*, on their way to a fancy dress party given by Mr. and Mrs. Donald Ogden Stewart in Hollywood.

Phyllis, Fred Junior, and Ava.

Fred, Ava, Fred Junior, and Phyllis.

Phyllis Astaire with her black Labrador.

Fred, Phyllis, and Fred Junior, with Phyllis's older son, Peter Potter.

Stanley Donen

I knew Phyllis. She was quiet, and not easily friendly, to me at least. She was friendly to Niven. She was small. It was a wonderful love story: She was married to somebody else, and Fred chased her all around the world, even stopped working, I think. He wanted her desperately, and was determined he was going to have her. And he bloody well got her. She was attractive, not beautiful. Very elegant.

Jean Howard

Linda Porter, Cole's wife, used to lunch with Phyllis, just the two of them. Phyllis wasn't social at all, although she came from a very good family in New York, more of a sort of snobbish family than Fred did. It wasn't just Hollywood. Phyllis was shy in New York also. Linda Porter certainly found Hollywood not to her taste at all. She was very simple, but she couldn't put up with Hollywood either.

Ava Astaire

I don't think Mummy ever liked show business. I found a diary of hers from when she first went out to Hollywood. It read something like, "Played tennis with the Marx brothers, but I can't say I like Hollywood very much." When we were growing up, we had a ranch in the San Fernando Valley where we spent every weekend until my mother died. There Daddy would garden and paint fences and do the general fixing of things. After Mummy died, we never went back.

Jean Howard

Phyllis dressed almost dowdy—I mean, nothing splashy, very simple. She was always thin. I think she smoked a lot. He didn't smoke. Phyllis was a very private person. She was very good-looking, she had beautiful manners, and she was insanely jealous of Fred. He wasn't allowed to kiss Ginger Rogers. I don't think Phyllis needed to worry, because I don't think Fred wanted to kiss Ginger Rogers anyhow, or anybody else.

Jeanne Vanderbilt

Phyllis was very positive, strong. A tiny little person. She did all of the tax returns, she ran the ranch, she ran the house. Fred counted on her very much, and was devastated when she died. I asked Fred about his romance with Barrie Chase after that, but he said she was too young.

Ginger Rogers

His wife was very sedate. She impressed everybody with her desire for Astaire to be minus any feminine attraction in any film.

Alfred Vanderbilt

In the old days, there were a bunch of us who were bachelors in Hollywood—Hank Fonda, Jimmy Stewart, Niven, Cary Grant, and Josh Logan, all more or less the same age. Almost always, when you were invited out to dinner, you were asked to bring a date—*except* at Fred and Phyllis's. One was never asked to bring a girl. Phyllis was extremely jealous.

Slim Keith

My then husband, Leland Hayward, was Fred's agent for many years. He dealt mostly with Phyllis, who was very businesslike. She kept Fred on a tight rein. She was very possessive, and I think she felt that since Ginger was certainly the best partner he ever had, and that he had such pleasure dancing with Ginger—there has to be something that sets up between two people who are flying through the air with the greatest of ease. There was never any evidence of anything. His manner and conduct were in general immaculate. But Phyllis always knew exactly where he was. If she played golf, he played with her. She was very much the lady at the head of the whole thing.

Cyd Charisse

Yes, I knew Phyllis. She was a charming woman, absolutely wonderful. He was broken over Phyllis's death.

Leslie Caron

Fred's wife was desperately ill during our rehearsals, and then she died. Fred used to sit down during a rehearsal and put his face in his towel and just cry. He would say, "Well, she's fighting, she's fighting. And we're hoping."

Jamie Niven

There was then a place in California called the Tower of Prayer that you could call, and there were prayers said on their broadcast for the successful recovery of Phyllis Astaire. I remember the night she died, because Daddy came in to tell us. He was very, very upset, very unhappy, because he really loved them both dearly, and he knew what pain Fred was suffering.

David Niven, Jr.
I remember I was in Paris with Daddy when Fred called and said that Phyllis had died.

Robert Wagner
Fred was absolutely crushed when his first wife, Phyllis, died.

Hermes Pan
It nearly killed Fred when Phyllis died. He was right in the middle of *Daddy Long Legs,* and he kept on working, which was probably good for him. He used to say, "My main happiness in life is coming home from work and seeing Phyllis."

Bill Self
I think Fred was in love with Phyllis all his life. I always felt that he was dating later for companionship and fun, nothing serious.

Dominick Dunne
I never knew Phyllis, but she certainly had an incredible influence on their life. After her death, she continued to be talked about all the time in Hollywood. Always respectfully.

Rocky Converse
Phyllis was the love of his life, there's no doubt about that.

Sam Goldwyn, Jr.
When Phyllis died, Fred built himself a new house. He never really left his family. He had his mother, he had his sister, he had his wife, Phyllis, and he had Ava. Ava filled the gap after her mother died.

Fred and Phyllis dancing at the Trocadero, Hollywood, October 1939.

HIS DAUGHTER, AVA

Ava Astaire McKenzie in Ireland,
July 1987.

Ava Astaire, the youngest of Fred's children, was born March 28, 1942. She was twelve when her mother died, and from then on she was her father's companion and hostess. She was also his colleague when she worked on the production of his TV specials in the 1970s. In 1966 she married Carl Bostleman, who owned a Hollywood decorating shop. She and Carl divorced three years later, and in 1970 she married her childhood sweetheart, Richard McKenzie, who was by then a widower with two small sons. Until 1981, when Fred married for the second time, the McKenzies spent part of each year living with him in his Beverly Hills house. Since then, they have divided their time between Ireland and Pennsylvania.

Fred and Ava Astaire in Paris after the making of *Funny Face*, 1956.

In Ireland in the late 1970s.

Fred and Ava at her coming-out dance in Hollywood, in the late 1950s.

Mrs. Sammy Davis, Jr.

He loved Ava absolutely. She was his ice cream and cake.

Audrey Hepburn

Fred adored Ava, that I do know.

Leonard Gershe

I first met Ava at a party Shirley and Flobe Burden gave for Geraldine Chaplin. Ava was a plump little thing, but she's grown into a beauty. She's radiant now, lovely, lovely, and warm and bright. I love her and her husband Richard together. They were very close to Fred. He adored Richard.

Ava Astaire

I was twelve when my mother died, so Daddy was both mother and father to me. We did everything together. We lived in Beverly Hills, and I had a governess to whom I was very close. She had also been very close to my mother, so that was all wonderful. We didn't go on family holidays, and after Mummy died we didn't do much about Christmas, which didn't bother me at all. My grandmother was alive, and Daddy would quite often go and spend Christmas with her in New York. She later came out to live with us in California. Family holidays with Mummy would mean going to the ranch. Before we had the one in the San Fernando Valley, we went to one near San Diego.

I have a half brother, Pete. He was four years old when Mummy and Daddy were married. Daddy always considered him a son. Pete is now retired. He was a policeman, and then later on in the Santa Barbara sheriff's department. I suppose I acted as Daddy's hostess, horrible little kid that I was. I went to a private school in Los Angeles that allowed children of movie people in; Candice Bergen and Alan Ladd's daughter, Alana, were there. My brother, Fred, went to public school. He also went to one or two boarding schools.

Bill Self

I used to see a lot of Fred Junior when he lived here, but he moved away when he remarried. He was a wonderful young man. My wife and I were moving, in the early days, and Fred Junior brought a truck over and loaded the furniture. He was a very nice guy. I think he was intimidated by his father's reputation. He didn't dare dance. Fred would have liked him to get into the business, and got him involved in *On the Beach*. He went to Australia and had a small job on the movie.

Ava and Fred Astaire.

Hermes Pan
Fred Junior hated show business. He had a ranch up north.

Roddy McDowall
His son Fred Junior was in Italy with him when we were making *The Midas Run,* and the three of us were really close. I like Fred Junior very much, although I haven't seen him in years.

Ava Astaire
Freddie and Pete often came to visit Daddy. Freddie would come down from where he lived. Especially over Daddy's last few months, he would go every few weeks. One of the last things Daddy said to me was "Freddie's great, isn't he? Just great."

Carol Lynley
We went to the Bistro a lot at one point, and one night I didn't notice an empty space and I fell off my chair into a black hole, at the most important table in the Bistro. I screamed as I fell, and found myself on the floor. Now, Fred has these enormous hands, and they came down and dragged me back up onto the chair, and during all this time he never stopped talking to me. The whole restaurant was mesmerized by my scream, but Fred just talked on as though nothing had happened. When I thanked him and told him how embarrassed I was, he told me this story about Ava going to dinner with him at Chasen's when she was about twelve. As she stood up to leave the table, her skirt fell off.

Ava Astaire
Richard, my husband, and I met when I was nineteen, in 1961, and we were together until I was twenty-one. Then I married somebody else, and then three years later we got back together again. Richard and I lived four months of the year with Daddy, and we traveled together. When we moved to Ireland, we used to stay with Daddy for three months every year. Then my grandmother died, and he used to say, "Can you stay a little longer?" and soon we were staying for four months.

Eleanor Lambert
Fred came to Ireland to make *The Purple Taxi* when I was staying with Sybil Connelly, the great Irish designer. He and Ava came to dinner.

Ava at home with her Elvis Presley records, in the 1950s.

Ava and Fred in Japan.

At home in Beverly Hills, 1959.

Richard McKenzie, Ava's husband.

Sir Robert Throckmorton
The last time I saw Fred was about 1976, in London. I went to have dinner with him and his daughter and her husband, at the Connaught.

Dominick Dunne
My whole acquaintance—as opposed to friendship—with Fred Astaire was through Ava. She was a friend of my wife's and mine, and she was a very interesting figure, very unlike the other daughters of Hollywood, like Louis B. Mayer's daughters and the Balaban heiress—all those girls. Ava's orientation was quite different from that of movie society. When she came out, she had a party at Romanoff's, but she was also a member of Las Madrinas. Now, nobody from the movies ever got into Las Madrinas before Ava. It was a cotillion for debutantes, for the old Los Angeles families. I can't remember how I first met her, but I have pictures in my scrapbook of her first marriage, to Carl Bostleman. The wedding was at night, at home, and it was Episcopal. She looked ravishing, all in cream-colored satin and rose-point lace. There was something so beautiful about Fred and Ava as he walked her up the room. Very moving. Ava seemed old beyond her years. I don't mean that badly; it was just that after her mother died, she assumed an important role in her father's life. She took care of him and understood him. She was young, yet she seemed like thirty.

Bill Self
The nicest part of his house is the wing he built for Ava. Fred's own bedroom was quite small and Spartan, very much a man's bedroom, unfrilly, simple, a few golf clubs stacked in the corner, a piano that he used to tinker with.

Ava Astaire
He kept the house the way it looked when Mummy was alive. And then we built a new house together, a wing for him and a wing for me. I had a wonderful marble step-down bath with an overhead shower, and as a surprise Daddy had it replaced with a regular porcelain tub and a telephone shower, because he thought that was more modern. Oh dear, my fabulous marble shower. I had to go into the guest room from then on to take a shower.

Sam Goldwyn, Jr.
I would imagine that he needed somebody after Ava left, to look after him. Robyn probably filled that function.

Richard McKenzie's portrait of Fred and his dog Allison, painted in 1987.

In Ireland in the late 1970s.

HIS SECOND WIFE, ROBYN

In 1973 Fred met his second wife, the jockey Robyn Smith, at the Santa Anita racetrack. They were introduced by Fred's old friend Alfred Vanderbilt, for whom Robyn raced horses. Robyn was born in 1944. After an unsuccessful start in an acting career, she became a jockey and rode her first race in 1969. She gave up racing after she married Fred, on June 24, 1980. She was thirty-five, and Fred was eighty-one.

Fred with his second wife, Robyn, "the jockey," in 1985.

Ava Astaire

Robyn took very good care of Daddy when he needed it the most, and I will always be grateful.

Hermes Pan

I didn't think Fred would ever marry again. And then one night over dinner he told me that he was in love. I think marrying Robyn prolonged his life eight years.

Alfred Vanderbilt

I introduced Robyn to Fred. She rode for me. She's a good jockey. Robyn could charm anybody. She used to say that what she really was good at was old men. And she was right. I suppose she was after security and prestige.

Mrs. Jock Whitney

Fred brought Robyn Smith to see us for a visit before they married, and he was very happy.

Irving "Swifty" Lazar

He didn't have any girlfriends, none at all. Robyn Smith, whom he married, was a very lovely girl. She was an athlete. Fred owned horses, and she was a jockey. She married him very late in life. He was eighty-one when he married her and eighty-eight when he died, so she had seven years. She had to take good care of him. I admire her for sticking it out.

Bill Self

I used to see much more of him before he married Robyn, which is natural.

Jockey Robyn, Smith.

Carol Lynley

Robyn and Fred definitely loved each other. One day when Fred was seventy-nine, we were having dinner at the Bistro, and he told me he was in love and planned to get married. My only argument with Robyn was that when they got married I didn't get to see so much of him, although I talked to him on the phone. I was a very tight friend of Fred all through the seventies. The last time I saw him was about nine months before he died. I had lost my handbag, and I get up very early, like Fred does. The telephone rang at about 6 A.M., and it was Robyn saying that they had my lost handbag. Some kid had found it on the side of the street, and had opened up the address book and found A for Astaire on the first page, so he had got on his bike and delivered it to Fred's house. Fred didn't like getting old, and he didn't get old until he was eighty-four. It made him cranky, which he always was anyway. His mother lived with him until she died, and I used to say how great it was that he came from a line of longevity, to which he would answer, "What's the use, if all you do is fall down and break your hip?" That is what his mother did.

I do believe that he and Robyn genuinely loved each other. The morning he got married he called me and said they were off down to a justice of the peace. She'd lived with him for only two months before they got married. He was very strict about that because of the age difference. He didn't want to become a Groucho Marx situation, and he felt that by handling it the way he did he would prevent that, which he did. Fred was never exploited. No one ever exploited him. One of the reasons he married Robyn, he told me, was to protect her from that sort of thing.

Leonard Gershe

I think that Robyn didn't want to compete with the memories that he shared with the rest of us. She changed the telephone number and didn't tell anyone. On Fred's birthday, Irving Berlin called to ask me for his telephone number. He'd never changed it since we'd known him, for thirty years. Poor Irving, who was ninety-nine, was trying to call Fred. His birthday is the day after Fred's.

Slim Keith

The last time I saw Fred was at Jock Whitney's funeral. He moved very slowly, and his wife was with him—the jockey. She sat in another room with Shipwreck Kelly and never spoke to anyone else. Shipwreck said to me, "You must talk to this darling little girl." I think she gave Fred companionship and care in those last years, when the days must stretch on forever. Although his name was linked to many names during his celibate years, I don't think anything mattered until Robyn came along.

George Christy

I would see Fred Astaire in restaurants like the Bistro with his wife, Robyn, who tended after him constantly. You couldn't want a better helpmate. I was very impressed with her devotion and loyalty. Very often they'd be dining with Hermes Pan, one of his favorite people.

Mrs. Oscar Levant

I like Robyn. She comes on very straightforward. She's without guile, without airs, very simply dressed, no makeup, no jewelry, good-looking, quite tall for a jockey. A few years after Fred's marriage to Robyn, Alfred Vanderbilt came to Los Angeles, and Alfred, Fred, Robyn, and I had dinner at Ma Maison. Robyn ordered for Fred. She took complete, efficient charge of him. I was rather pleased to see her take this kind of care of Fred. I knew Fred adored her. Another night, before Fred and Robyn were married, Henry Ephron and Fred and I went to Trader Vic's. Fred looked so rejuvenated; I had a feeling he had had some work done. I feel certain he did. Fred and I had a Mai Tai. Robyn didn't show up. Fred said she was down at the track looking for a mount. He kept saying, "The poor girl can't find a mount." Fred started feeling good over the Mai Tai and began nudging up to me. He had changed a lot, I think, from being a reserved and standoffish person. He was warm and friendly. Robyn really devoted herself to him.

Bill Self

During the time he was married to Robyn, he used to get invited to receive awards in England, he used to get invited to the White House, but he just didn't feel up to it anymore.

Dr. Harry Reizner

The last time I saw Fred was when Robyn called me and said that she knew that I didn't make house calls, but it was a bit hard for Fred to get over to the office. So that next Saturday I went up to the house and took care of Fred, and then Fred and Robyn and I sat at the breakfast table, a round table near the window. His mind was clear, though he was physically weak. One thing I noticed was that there was a great deal of love and affection from Robyn. She never got in nurses or attendants. She stood right there beside him.

Howard W. Koch

I knew Robyn from the racetrack. She's a lady. I see her walking early in the morning now, very blue, very down. It was a great love affair.

Robyn Smith with Alfred Vanderbilt, 1972.

HIS PRIVATE WORLD

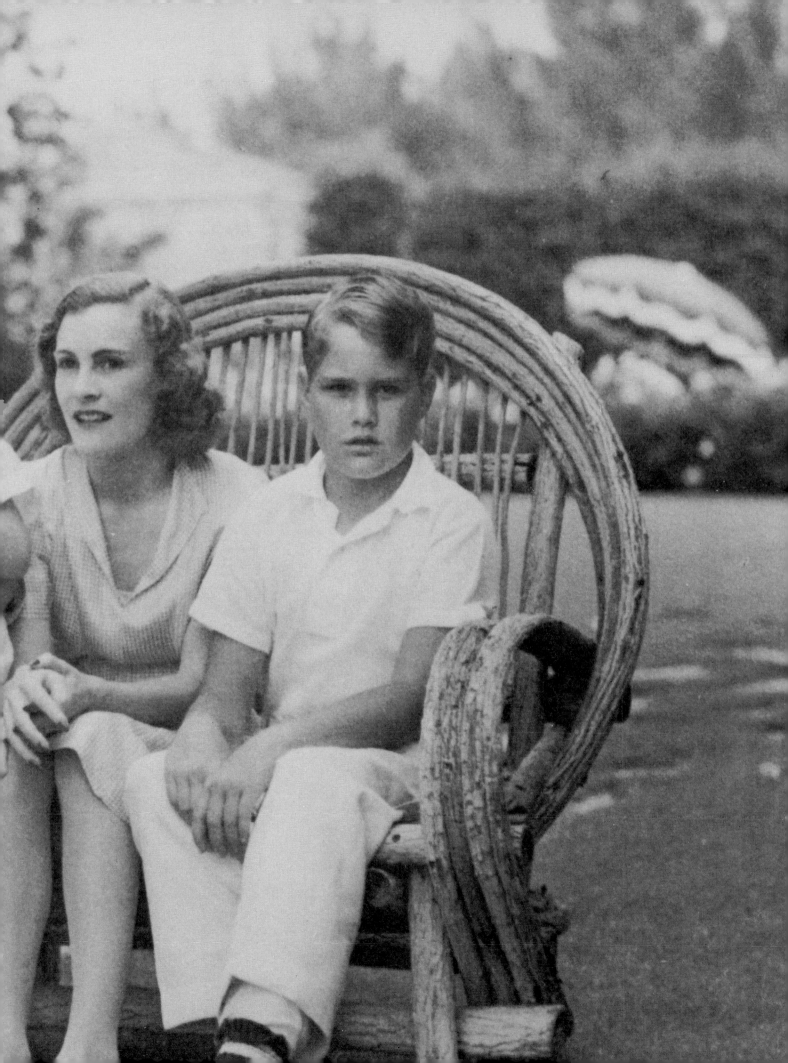

HIS DAILY ROUTINE

f Fred's stardom was based on hard work, his private life was centered on simple routine. He was a genuine family man, and he put a great premium on privacy. He traveled only when his work necessitated it, and he chose to devote his free time to a small, selective group of friends.

Overleaf: Fred, Fred Junior, Phyllis, and Peter in 1939.   **Relaxing before making *Top Hat*, 1935.**

Ava Astaire

Daddy always woke up early—three or four. Then he'd do all the crossword puzzles.

Tina Sinatra

You could set your clock by Fred's morning walk down Beverly Drive. At nine o'clock he was walking to his office.

Carol Lynley

I used to talk to him at six-thirty in the morning. When I would go out with him, we'd get back to his house at about nine-thirty. We'd go into the fabulous bar area and have a nightcap, and then I'd leave.

Dominick Dunne

He was a great wanderer in Beverly Hills, at least on Saturdays. I would often see him walking down the street, with that wonderful walk, in those extraordinary clothes. Nobody ever stopped him; there was something aloof about him. Yet if you did make eye contact with him, he would chat. My conversations with him were generally about Ava. That's probably why I always think of him as a father, and there ain't nothing in my book nicer to look at than a father and daughter who adore each other. And they related to each other in the best possible way that a father and daughter can: They were proud of each other.

At home in Beverly Hills, 1959.

Jo Cody

I had a friend who was a cook at Mr. Astaire's, and one day she told me that he needed a housekeeper and asked me if I'd be interested in the job. I thought, Well, I'll go and see him anyway; there's nothing to lose. Of course, I liked him right away; he was so sweet. And I guess he liked me, because he hired me. I was the housekeeper, and there was always a cook too. His mother had just passed away, maybe six months before. We got on very well, the two of us. He was the gentlest man I've ever known. I never, never, never heard him say one bad word against anybody—really, I swear to God—not in front of me anyway, in the eight years I lived there and worked for Mr. A. I used to have to watch myself, because when you say you live in, it has a kind of a different meaning here! I was born in Ireland, and every year he would always buy my ticket to go home to Ireland. He didn't have to do that. He would ask me not to tell anyone he was doing it. If he did something for you, he didn't let the whole world know, which is rather nice. One year, I'd just gotten back from Ireland, and I got a call to say that my mother was pretty ill, and he was so good. He called up the travel agent right away and got me a ticket to go home, and he called the limousine service, and he called a friend of his at TWA and asked if he would watch out for me. He would always tell me to call collect when I was telephoning from Ireland. I come from a small town, Kilkenny, and my brothers and sisters didn't have a phone, so I would go to a public box and I'd call up the operator and ask to make a collect call to Fred Astaire. The operator hung up! So I called back and said I was wanting to make this call, and they hung up again! I called a third time and said, "Don't you dare hang up on me again." They thought somebody was playing a joke. I finally got through, and Mr. A. thought it was hilarious when I told him.

He always had his breakfast around a quarter to eight. He would be up earlier, but he was very considerate to the people that worked for him. He didn't want to have us start too early. Then he'd potter around, go down to the post office and collect his mail. He ate like a bird, a very simple breakfast. I wish I had the discipline he had. Sometimes when the cook had fixed something he liked, he would have liked to have had some more, but he would never do so. He would have a scrambled egg, juice, and coffee. He always had his lunch at twelve-thirty. He always had soup for lunch and maybe a hot dog or a sandwich. He loved homemade soup and had it twice a day, for lunch and for dinner. He would eat any kind of soup so long as it was homemade. And then our soaps used to come on. We watched "The Guiding Light" and "As the World Turns." He would watch television in his room, and I would watch it in mine, and at the end we'd come into the hall to discuss it. We'd argue about who was doing what and who was going to do what. Then, if the racing was on, he would go to Hollywood Park or to Santa Anita, or he'd go to visit his friends—he didn't do a lot, really.

On Sunday, Bill Self used to come over, and they would play cards. Hermes Pan was a regular visitor, and Randolph Scott, and Robert Wagner—who was always very charming and nice, which they all were—and David Niven, and Douglas Fairbanks, Jr., and Carol Lynley. Michael Jackson used to call up quite a bit, so I talked to him on the phone often.

Mr. A. would always have his supper at six-thirty. He was a very simple man. Always soup, veggies, maybe some steak or chicken or a lamb chop, and a little dessert, like ice cream, nothing fancy. The cook and I would leave him after he'd finished dinner, which was seven or a little after, and we wouldn't see him again until morning. He wouldn't have a lot of people in. He'd go out with his friends sometimes, and he'd always let us know a week ahead. I used to go and check on him before he went out, to see he had remembered and was getting ready. One night, he'd said he was going out, so the cook and I had our dinner, and then I went to check on Mr. A. He was eating potato chips at the bar and having a little drink, so I said to him, "Now, you'd better not eat all that junk food, or you'll not be able to eat your dinner when you go out." He said, "But I'm not going out." I said, "What do you mean, you're not going out? You told me you were going out." He told me his friends had canceled, but he said, "I didn't want to disturb anybody. I didn't want to put anybody out." Can you believe it? Here he is, eating potato chips, just because he didn't want to tell us that he had had a change of plans. I told him that I was going to ask the cook to fix him something, and he said, "No, no, no." After a lot of persuasion, he agreed to have something very simple, like some soup and a sandwich. He was so considerate. His sister used to come and visit us and stay a couple of weeks. She was a lot of fun, and Mr. A. loved having her around. She was different from him, not at all quiet and shy. She told a lot of jokes. There was a marvelous gardener, Luis, who was with Mr. A. for years and years and years. Mr. A. had a business manager named Harold Williams, and a secretary called Betty, who did all the bills for the house. Betty Johns. He never took exercise; he didn't need it, he was so thin. He took up going around on a skateboard until he had the accident, and that was exercise, I guess. He was

Skateboarding at home in the late 1970s.

seventy-something when he started, and he was marvelous at it. The skateboard was his grandson's, Fred Junior's son's, and he left it behind one time when he was over. I used to stand out in the driveway and watch Mr. A., but this day I wasn't there to keep an eye on him and make sure he didn't do anything that he shouldn't do. He came in the house shouting, "Jo, Jo, Jo!" He said he thought he'd broken his wrist, and I thought he was joking, because we often used to play jokes on each other. But then the whole wrist swelled up, so we drove down to Dr. Kurland's office, way down in Inglewood. He had a cast on for about six weeks.

Mr. A. didn't always close the garage door at night, and one April Fool's Day I remember going in to him and asking him how he'd got home last night. He said, "What do you mean, 'How did you get home?' " I told him that the car wasn't in the garage. He looked at me astounded, and dashed out the front door. I shouted after him, "April Fool!" Sometimes he would tell me someone was on the phone who wasn't on the phone. He was a fun tease. He always went to church on Sundays. I went to the Good Shepherd, and he went to the one next door. People used to come up to the house asking to see Mr. Astaire, and he tried to see as many people as he could, but he couldn't see all of them; anyway, one day we were both at the front door and I saw the people before he did, so I suggested to him that he get out through the side door, and with that he just backed out the other way, and I shouted, "That's all right, James." So the people never knew. He didn't like to upset people.

He used to like to potter around the garden, and one day he decided to paint the water faucets red to make them more identifiable. It was a windy day, and he had a spray can of red paint, and he came back into the house really pleased with himself, saying "I've done a great job. Now Luis can find exactly where the water faucets are." I said, "That's great, but now take a look at your shirt." He'd sprayed himself all over. It was one of his good shirts, too. I had to scold him. He tried very hard to be handy around the house, no matter what I'd ask him to do, but I don't think he had much training in that line. Mr. A. was the one who started calling me Jo. My real name is Joanna. I could sit down and talk to Mr. A. about most things. If there was ever anything wrong with my car, he would tell me to take it down to his man and get it fixed, and he would take care of the bill. He also gave me his credit card for the gas. Locally, I never had any trouble, but I did stop once for gas on Sunset, and when I took out the credit card, they said, "Well, you don't look like Fred Astaire." I only used the

After falling off the skateboard.

Playing ball with his black Labrador.

card locally from then on.

Ava had a special area at the end of the house, with her own entrance, a nice sitting room and bedroom. She takes after her father. She is always so down to earth, so friendly, and she makes everyone feel welcome. She's great. Fred Junior would come to the house, but not often; he was always pleasant. His stepson, Peter, would come also. When Mr. A. was doing *Purple Taxi,* he went to Paris and then to Ireland, and he used to call me up at least once a week. I had to keep notes on the soap operas. In fact, he was the one that got me addicted to them; I never watched soap operas until I went to Mr. A. When I used to go home to Ireland for a month, he would send me notes on what was happening in the soaps, which was very sweet of him, since I'm sure he had better things to do. He hated it if people didn't get along in the household, like the cook or the cleaning people or whatever.

He took care of his cleaning himself. He used to wash his socks, too, and his underwear. I asked him why, and he said he was used to doing it from when he was on the road. Some things, I guess, you can't get out of. He was a

very neat man. He always made his own bed. He didn't change it, but he would always make it. He preferred baths to showers. In the mornings, he was dressed by breakfast.

He had a dog, Allison; she was a cockapoo (a cross between a cocker spaniel and a poodle). I love animals, and I was great friends with Allison. He would take her down to the post office when she was younger. She'd jump in the car, and then when she got older, she couldn't hear so well, and since he didn't have her on a leash, he was afraid that she wouldn't be able to hear him and that she would get hurt. He had a cockatiel also, called Gregory, after Gregory Peck, and also because the bird pecked.

Fred and Allison.

E. P. Varjian

He was a nice, soft-spoken gentleman, always pleasant. He would come almost every day, until the last years, at 11 A.M. His office was just around the corner. He had an account here at Premier Market. My uncle opened the place in 1939, and I started to deliver to Mr. Astaire in 1949. He used to come down here on his way to the races, with Danny, his driver, in a little Ranchero, and his mother used to come down here in a little black coat and a chauffeur-driven car. A cute little mother. He was very polite. He would allow anyone to go ahead of him at the checkout stand. Never pushy or demanding in any way. There weren't too many of this type of market, and so many of the stars came here. We still call ourselves Market of the Stars. We had Humphrey Bogart, Randolph Scott . . . Mr. Astaire was indecisive. I had to help him with his Christmas presents. He'd worry about whether he was sending too much or too little. He'd buy potato chips and tomato juice drinks. He'd go over to the potato chip rack and spend a few minutes over there. He liked to be here when there weren't too many people around.

Ava Astaire

What did I think Daddy did? I just knew, because I was taken to the studio. Much later, of course, I realized that not everyone does that. The question I am most often asked is, What was it like growing up as the child of a movie star? But not having had anything else, I didn't honestly think anything was different from anyone else's life, except for when we were traveling, and then life seemed much more social, more show biz. Daddy and I traveled together a lot. He took me to Lismore the first summer after Mummy died, and then a couple of years later to Tokyo and Hong Kong, because *Silk Stockings* was opening in Hong Kong. And in between I went to France to be with him straight after he finished *Funny Face*.

Fred with his two cockatiels.

Tina Sinatra

When Robert Wagner and I stopped dating, Fred and I didn't. There was never any romance, but we would spend at least ten nights a month having dinner together, just the two of us. He liked to talk, and we would spend hours talking. He was very gentlemanly. He would always come and pick me up. I lived in Century City then. We'd go to La Scala, Dan Tana's, Chasen's, the Bistro. We'd get dressed up, the two of us. We used to go to movies at twelve o'clock in the afternoon. He would wear dark glasses and put his collar up. One night we went somewhere a little more public than usual, and our picture was taken. It ran on the cover of the recently resurrected *National Enquirer.* Above the picture they ran a caption: "Who is the mystery woman in Fred Astaire's life?"

Caspar of the Bistro

Fred Astaire came in over the years with pretty much the same people: his family, his wife, Hermes Pan. Never, for the most part, more than four people. He would come in around seven o'clock. He'd sit at the same table, a little one in the corner, because it had privacy. I've been here since opening day, about twenty-five years ago, so I knew Fred Astaire from that time on. In fact, I knew him from Chasen's, where I worked before. He was a beautiful man. This is a little neighborhood, so I'd bump into him at least three times a week, at the post office or whatever. He was pretty much a creature of habit. He didn't eat very much. He'd have a cocktail, like an old-fashioned. He always had a little seafood to start, a mixture of crab and shrimp, and a small Bistro salad. The Bistro salad is the heart of palm on a bed of tomato, and endive and mushrooms, with vinaigrette. Then he'd often have fresh calf's liver. He liked it cut very thin, with onions on the side, instead of having it smothered with onions. And he loved creamed spinach. He'd always have a cappuccino to finish up, with a little liqueur. He would always ring and book before he came. He didn't linger.

Irving "Swifty" Lazar

Fred was always working, and he never spent anything, so he must have left a lot of money.

Photograph dedicated by Fred to Betsy and Jock Whitney.

Fred Astaire's close friends could be counted on the fingers of two hands. He was intimate with a small group of colleagues he respected most, like Hermes Pan, and a few lifelong friends who shared his interest in sports and racing, like Alfred Vanderbilt, Jock Whitney, and Bill Self. He and his first wife, Phyllis, were part of a select, unostentatious set who were considered the best of the Old Hollywood, including the Cole Porters, the Irving Berlins, the Samuel Goldwyns, the David Nivens, the Douglas Fairbankses, and the Gregory Pecks. Later Fred chummed with a few younger colleagues like Robert Wagner and Carol Lynley.

Fred and Phyllis Astaire with Randolph Scott.

Paintings of Fred Astaire by his friend Irving Berlin, done in 1973.

Irving Berlin

As a talent Fred Astaire was pure gold, and as a friend no one came closer.

Cyd Charisse

Fred had his special group of people that he enjoyed being with, and it would be on a very rare occasion that you would see him at a large affair.

The Rajmata of Jaipur

I met Fred Astaire once at a dinner party given by Zsa Zsa Gabor. This was about 1984 or 1985. I was staying with Cyd Charisse and Tony Martin, and it was Cyd who introduced me to Fred Astaire. I remember that the rest of the evening Fred Astaire stayed with Cyd Charisse. He said she was his favorite partner.

Peter Duchin

Jock Whitney was the most wonderful, cuddly individual—and funny! He was the warmest man—you just wanted to hug him the moment you saw him. Astaire basked in that and loved him. He admired Jock a lot, not because he had money, but because of the way he was. Also, Jock dressed extremely well, as Fred did. Fred probably tried to emulate him.

Alfred Vanderbilt

I think Jock was his best friend. He knew the Guests, Winston and Raymond, well. Dorothy Fell and her sister-in-law Fifi Fell were great friends of Phyllis, because they were the right sort of girls to have around.

Ava Astaire

Monsignor Jim was a janitor at MGM before he became a priest. Hermes Pan, who was a Catholic, got him a job cleaning Daddy's dressing room, and soon after he started, Daddy asked him and his wife out to dinner with the Alfred Vanderbilts. Jim was about twenty-eight, and had to borrow a suit to go out that evening. During dinner, Jim was asked what he did, and I don't think people believed him when he said, "I'm a janitor." Then he turned to Daddy and said, "And you've got to start picking up your beer tops, because it's adding to my work." Daddy always drank Heineken.

Jean Howard

Fred was very fond of David Niven. And Douglas Fairbanks was a great friend. There was nothing snob or social-climbing about Fred. If he liked Jock Whitney, it was based on horses, not because of Jock's money. Like Cole Porter, Fred Astaire was selective about people.

David Niven, Jr.

As far as Daddy was concerned, Fred was like his older brother. There were eleven years between them. Daddy would literally not come to California without seeing Fred. Fred was a total class act, and both Fred and Daddy had that. They didn't talk about show business; it was a job. If you're a plumber, you don't go home and talk about it.

Jamie Niven

Daddy thought Fred was the best man in town. He said that Fred was the most important relationship he had when he was in Hollywood.

Ava Astaire

Frances Goldwyn was a very close friend of my mother, and they went there a lot. And Cole Porter was their close friend, and the Berlins, so they did mix, but then it certainly wasn't the way it is now. There was the old Hollywood, and there's the new one. Thank God most of the old aren't around anymore: They would be so shocked at what it's like now.

Jean Howard

At the Goldwyns' there'd be Robert Sherwood, there'd be Irving Berlin, the Porters. That's definitely the old and best Hollywood. They weren't parties, they were just dinners. Hollywood was like that—there were groups, and they never mixed. The Warners gave the parties, and Clifton Webb gave great parties, and David Selznick. But not Frances Goldwyn. That's why the Astaires liked her. They knew it would be eight people only. Ginger was never in the groups that I knew. On Saturday nights we had parties, and everybody got drunk—not the women, but the guys did. You'd never find Phyllis and Fred Astaire at those parties.

Jeanne Vanderbilt

It was nice to go to dine at the Astaires' because it was like home—not like the other Hollywood homes. Dinner would be served as soon as we arrived, always seven-thirty for eight. There'd always be a movie afterward. There'd always be a maid with a black uniform and a white apron.

The Astaire family celebrating Adele's eightieth birthday, September 10, 1977.

Fred, Mr. and Mrs. Fred Junior, Ava and Richard McKenzie, Adele, Mr. and Mrs. Peter Potter.

Don Cook

I think he enjoyed coming to my house because there were never more than ten people. Leonard Gershe would come, and Betty White and Allen Ludden, and Ava and Richard, of course. One night I was going out with Stefanie Powers, and Ava and Dick were joining us. It was black tie. We went up to Fred's house for a drink first. Fred would usually stay in his part of the house on these occasions. But this time, all of a sudden he comes puffing out. Ava told me later that he'd been dying to meet Stefanie Powers. Well, Stefanie, who'd never met him, was absolutely enthralled. And she was a good pool player, so they shot some pool together.

Katharine Hepburn

I wasn't really a friend of Freddy's; I hardly knew him. We were just both at RKO. Obviously I admired him wildly, as who didn't? George Cukor and I loved to go to all his previews and froth at the mouth with wild jealousy. He was just an extraordinary creature, I think. I think I admired him too much to know him. He was a very, very good friend of Leland Hayward and of friends of mine, but I didn't really know Freddy. I never worked with him, but we worked sort of side by side at a time when there was a sort of friendly atmosphere at RKO, and one knew everyone. We both kept ourselves to ourselves. We had this great respect for each other, which we were never to lose.

Ginger Rogers

I think if you knew Fred Astaire you knew he was making an effort to climb up that avenue of life. Did he love to mix with people who were wellborn? Of course. He loved to have them around. They would come to visit him on the set, but I don't remember their names.

Hermes Pan

I used to go and see them sometimes at their ranch in Escondido, and people would drop in—like Gable would occasionally, and David Niven—and we'd go hunting for quail and horseback riding.

Visiting David Niven in the South of France.

With Michael Jackson.

Bill Self

I first met him in New York in 1950, with Spencer Tracy. He was a buddy of mine—he preceded Fred as my buddy—and we did a lot together. We traveled together. Spence asked me to go to New York with him, because he said I didn't talk too much. We went on the train, and on the train were Fred Astaire and his wife. We went to the diner on the first evening, and there they were. So Spence introduced us. When Fred and I remet in 1957, Fred remembered our first meeting.

Carol Lynley

I have a tendency to gush, and I loved him dearly. He was very much a father figure to me. We dated and carried on, or rather didn't carry on—we didn't have an affair. He would have liked to, but I couldn't do it.

Tina Sinatra

Was Fred lonely after Phyllis died? He filled his time. Danny, his chauffeur, was very close to him. So was the wardrobe person he shared with Robert Wagner. Fred disliked big groups. It was usually one on one. I was flattered that he and Hermes would want me to join them. Fred liked youth, and to be around young people. I never got the picture that Fred was part of the Hollywood scene. Fred was a gypsy.

Carol Lynley

Fred was very much a day-to-day person, and he hated nostalgia with a passion. He was very current. He had phone calls daily from Michael Jackson—a long telephone relationship.

Sam Goldwyn, Jr.

Tony Curtis was a good friend of his. They used to play pool together.

Mrs. Sammy Davis, Jr.

Sammy and I used to go to his house for dinner. We could just walk down the hill. I was enamored of him. One day I told him I'd love one of his shoes, and he gave me one for my special birthday. Sammy always adored him. Ava got Sammy Fred's suit from *The Band Wagon*. They were both the same size—light, not fragile, just light, and very strong. Sammy never wore Fred's suit—he wouldn't dare.

Jean Howard

Fred played a lot of golf with his buddy Randolph Scott. They were great, great friends.

Mrs. Oscar Levant

In the old days, Fred and Phyllis didn't socialize much. They saw Ellen and Irving Berlin, Frances Goldwyn. They all liked Oscar because we didn't really socialize.

Don Cook

Gregarious is not a word you associate with Fred Astaire.

Mrs. Lester Holt

If Fred didn't like you, in subtle little ways, he let you know it. He was very fond of Robert Wagner and Tina Sinatra.

Irving "Swifty" Lazar

Fred was very friendly with Leland Hayward, who was his agent.

Leonard Gershe

He wasn't at all social, although I've seen him at parties, like at Gregory and Veronique Peck's. Fred Astaire stood for class. Dellie married an English lord. Phyllis was a socialite. She was the niece of Henry Bull. All their friends here, like the Burdens, were very social. Fifi Fell was Ava's godmother. I met Fifi Fell years ago with the Kennedys. She was friendly with Jack and with Pat. Fred spoke the same language as all those people. He had this innate classiness.

Hermes Pan

His closest friends were Randy Scott, Bill Self, David Niven, and I. Jock Whitney was a very close friend, as was Liz Whitney. He was very popular in London, and he was catered to by the royalty.

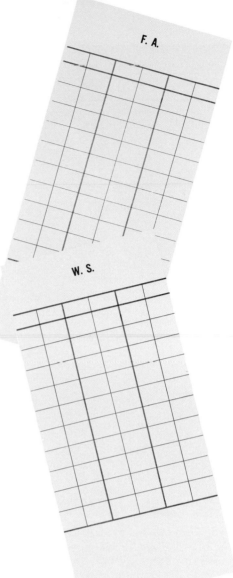

Bill Self and Fred Astaire's gin rummy scorecards.

Gin rummy settlement.

Bill Self and Fred Astaire during one of their Sunday afternoon gin rummy sessions.

Judy Garland and Fred Astaire at the MGM Silver Anniversary Luncheon, February 1949.

With Patricia Neal.

Bill Self

I certainly always considered myself one of his best friends. Strangely, he didn't cross-pollinate his friends. I was never with Fred and Gregory Peck, or Bob Wagner. My life with Fred was very private and personal. We got to know each other at the Bel Air Country Club. One day I went up there to play golf, but didn't have a game. The caddy master said that Mr. Astaire was there but that he was very shy. Anyway, he agreed to play with me, and we played for quite a while. He asked me if I was in television, and I said yes. He asked my advice about a show he'd been offered, but said he couldn't tell me the name of it. Now, it so happened that I'd been asked to produce a show with a major star whose name I'd not been allowed to know yet. So I asked Fred, "Is the show *The Father of the Bride*?" We both roared with laughter. In the end, neither of us did the show, but that was the start of our friendship. From then on, we played golf two or three times a week, and that drifted into gin rummy. Fred and I played gin rummy almost every Sunday, one o'clock to four o'clock. At his house or mine. We did lots of things together. We went to the fights together. Fred loved boxing.

We traveled together a little bit. We went to New York

With Carol Lynley.

a couple of times. On one of those trips, in the seventies, I asked Fred where he wanted to dine, and he said, "21." So I made a reservation, and we got there and were seated. Suddenly the manager came up to me and asked if Mr. Astaire was my guest, and when I said yes he moved us into the right room, where he knew Fred liked to sit.

Fred came to see me when I was sick in the hospital on and off for five years during the eighties. That was an enormous chore for him, because the UCLA medical center is a big complex, and parking is difficult. I was very pleased that he would bother. When he was in the hospital, at the end of his life, he didn't want to see anybody. Obviously, I think he knew he was dying.

Mervyn LeRoy, Clark Gable, and
Fred Astaire

Fred Astaire greeting Mick Jagger, Jerry Hall, and Ahmet Ertegun at the Kennedy Center.

With Lieutenant and Mrs. James Altemus at the Stork Club, New York.

Randy Scott, Phyllis and Fred Astaire, and Liz Whitney (the former Mrs. John Hay Whitney) dining in the Beverly Hills Brown Derby, December 1941.

Howard Hawks, Mrs. Samuel
Goldwyn, and Fred Astaire at Ciro's,
Beverly Hills, August 1941.

Mrs. Oscar Levant

My husband died suddenly, and it was a terrible shock. For
a few days I couldn't see anyone other than my daughters.
On the second night, I was sitting on the sofa with my
second daughter, Lana, and the doorbell rang. Lana said
she'd answer it, and I said I didn't want to see anyone.
When she came back she said, "Not even Fred Astaire?" I
said straight out, "Oh sure, I'll see him." He came in so
light-footed, as if he was on a cloud, and sat down next to
me. I could barely hear what he said, because he was
whispering, but I knew he was saying sympathetic things.
He knew what I was going through, because he'd been
through it with his wife. I told Fred that Oscar had spent a
lot of the last years in bed, and that the old Astaire movies
on television had cheered him up a lot.

Liza Minnelli

Fred took the time for his friends.

With Hermes Pan in Hollywood,
during the 1960s.

 e seemed to have a special way with children, not only his own children and grandchildren but also the children of his friends. He was always encouraging to them, and he enjoyed seeing them develop into the adults he had hoped and predicted they might become.

Teaching his son, Fred Junior, to dance, 1941.

Jamie Niven

I lived in Hollywood from 1945 until 1958. It was totally different from what it is now. In those days there were about fifty of us children of Hollywood parents who were friends. We all had English nannies and moved in a group. Daddy and Fred were both very much fathers to us children, which is more than can be said for a lot of the other parents.

David Niven, Jr.

When I started the restaurant Drones in London, I decided to hang famous movie stars' baby pictures on the walls. The first person I wrote to was Fred, and he was the first to respond, with a great baby picture of himself. I was probably three and a half when he first knew me. I remember looking forward to going out to the beautiful ranch they had in the San Fernando Valley. Actually, I think that was the first time I'd ever seen a live cow. Fred said, "Go with Ava and she'll show you how to milk the cows." I thought milk came from a bottle, not from a cow, but I went with Ava, who started pulling this great nipple and squirting me in the face with the milk. Of course, I screamed and went rushing in to Fred and Daddy, saying that this horrible, horrible girl has done this terrible thing to me.

Peter Duchin

I met Fred when I was about twelve, with my father, on Long Island, maybe with the Harrimans, the ones who are both dead. Dad was a pianist and orchestra leader, and they'd probably worked together. Fred was very interested in what I was doing. He wanted to know whether I played the piano.

Mrs. Oscar Levant

Fred came to the house one night, and Marsha, my eldest daughter, who was then eleven or twelve, had just started taking dance lessons. I said to her, "Guess who's coming tonight? Fred Astaire, to go over the numbers for the show." When the doorbell rang, Marsha rushed down the stairs and Oscar introduced them. He then suggested that Marsha do a dance for Fred, and she went shrieking out of the room and back upstairs.

Whitney Tower

Fred used to come to Aiken, South Carolina, to stay with the Bulls, his wife's aunt and uncle. The Bulls' house was right across the street from the house owned by my mother and stepfather, Flora Whitney and Cully Miller. Fred liked to play bridge, and when he was staying with the Bulls he used to come to our house to play bridge with my stepfather and other people. My mother didn't play. I was twelve years old in 1935, and my sister Pam and I had been to see *Top Hat* in the local town at least thirteen times. We knew every line spoken by every person in the film, and we were naturally avid Fred Astaire fans. So you can imagine how I felt when I heard not only that Fred Astaire was in town, but that he was coming to play cards at our house. I was home sick from the Aiken Preparatory boarding school, in bed with flu, and I said to my mother, "When he comes, would you bring him up to say hello?" And she did. I was in a brass bed, and he came up and said hello and asked me how I felt. I said, "Fine, but I'd feel better if you'd do me a favor." And he said, "What can I do?" I said, "Tap-dance for me once around this bed." Nothing ventured, nothing lost. And he said, "Of course. What would you like me to dance?" I said, "Anything from *Top Hat*. I've seen it thirteen times." And he danced right around the bed, not once but twice. Well, that's the sort of thing a child never forgets. Then he said, "Nice to see you," and away he went. My sister and I were so excited about this that within a week or so we told Mother that nothing would do but we had to learn tap dancing. She took a pair of my shoes and a pair of Pam's shoes and had taps put on them, and she discovered a tap dancing teacher in Augusta, Georgia, twenty miles away. She arranged for this person to come and teach us. My sister's friend's governess was a very amateur pianist, who knew one tune, "Shuffle Off to Buffalo," and she was told to sit at the piano and play while this poor unhappy dance teacher had to teach us. Before long, we had twenty of our friends with us learning to tap. We did this for a few months, until the end of the year, and then we dispersed, and that was the end of the tap dancing.

I didn't see Fred again until long after I'd become a racing correspondent for *Sports Illustrated*. It was in California, at Santa Anita. I'd just done a piece on the jockey Bill Shoemaker. Fred's trainer at the time was a wonderful man called Bill Winfrey. When Fred wasn't working, he used to go and have lunch in the Turf Club with Bill Winfrey and another friend of his, an orthopedic surgeon, who took care of athletes and jockeys, called Dr. Robert Kurland. I joined them. This was in the sixties, a long time after the episode in Aiken, South Carolina. I said, "You know, my stepfather, Cully Miller, was a great friend of Mr. Bull in Aiken, and my mother, Flora Whitney, remembers you with great fondness from your trips. They always say when I'm coming out here on assignment, 'If you see Fred, please give him our best.'" He said that he'd always remembered Aiken with such fondness that he'd sent his son to the Aiken Preparatory School. I asked him if he remembered going to play cards with Cully Miller one day and being asked to go upstairs and dance around a sick boy's bed. He said that he certainly remembered it, because the boy had said he'd seen *Top Hat* thirteen times. And I said, "I'm the boy." And he said, "Well, I'm so glad to meet you finally." It was so typical of Fred to turn something into a compliment to somebody else. He then said, "Why I really wanted to meet you is that I read with interest your pieces on Bill Shoemaker, who I think is the greatest jockey in the world. I'm so glad to meet the guy who wrote them." From then on we'd see each other occasionally at Santa Anita, and we always had things in common. He knew I was a cousin of his great friend Jock Whitney. He was just a wonderful, modest guy.

Fred Junior.

Robert Wagner
I got to know Fred Astaire when I was seven years old, because I went to school with his stepson, Peter. I was boarding at the school and I used to go and spend weekends at his house. Mr. Astaire would come on Friday afternoons and pick me up. He would lift me up and put me in the backseat. At seven, I didn't know who he was, but I remember vividly his caring for me, his feelings for me. My family lived near the golf course where he played regularly, so we would go out and play golf together early in the morning, nine holes. He knew I wanted to be an actor, and he used to say to me, "Go for it, boy, go for it." And he was endlessly encouraging when I did get started.

Roddy McDowall
I used to go and watch Fred rehearse when I was a child, but I never met him. Maybe I was too shy, because I was absolutely mesmerized by him. He was in the first movie I ever saw, which resulted with my falling in love with Irene Dunne and wanting to be Fred Astaire when I grew up. It was a film called *Roberta*—a hallmark in my life.

Ahmet Ertegun

I first met Fred Astaire when my brother and my sister and my mother and I went on a semiofficial invitation to Los Angeles. My father was the Turkish ambassador in Washington, and the American film industry was trying to promote itself abroad. We visited all the major studios where films were being made with big stars like Clark Gable. We had the great pleasure of visiting a set where Fred Astaire and Rita Hayworth were making a film. We had some photographs taken and chatted. He was my idol—the most elegant man. This was around 1940. At that time there were a couple of people whom I respected because of the way they looked and the way they behaved, who seemed to embody everything that was good about the elegance of the Western world: David Windsor, the Prince of Wales, and Fred Astaire.

Sam Goldwyn, Jr.

When I joined the army, I had to give a couple of references for a security check, and I put Mr. and Mrs. Fred Astaire because I couldn't think of anybody else who had known me that long. Later, people came around to check me out, and Mrs. Astaire called Mother and said, "I hope he's not in any trouble."

Leonard Gershe

I first met him when he was doing a film called *The Belle of New York* and I was out here with a stage musical called *Wedding Day. Wedding Day* became the movie *Funny Face* several years later, and it was during *Funny Face* that we got to know each other. I'd worked on a song called "Born in a Trunk" for Judy Garland in *A Star Is Born,* and sometimes I saw him with Judy. Then a few years ago, well, twelve or thirteen years ago, there was a place in L.A. called the Factory, which was the hot disco—owned by Anthony Newley. I went there with Liza and Mia to some charity thing. Fred was there, and Liza said, "Oh, it's Fred Astaire!" I thought she was going to lose her mind. He couldn't have been more darling, told her how he'd known her as a small child. This was well before he called her the Crown Princess of Hollywood in *That's Entertainment.* The next day she called me and asked me why Tiffany's didn't do a window for Fred Astaire. I asked her why, naturally, and Liza said, "For swellness."

Liza Minnelli

He always showed enormous pride in me—he was like family in that way, like my favorite uncle, who cares and comes to the school plays and things like that. I was like his favorite niece. He liked me, liked talking to me, because it was a nice transition from knowing somebody as a child. He was interested in art, and wanted to know what was going on on Broadway. I always felt he was interested in what I was doing. I think the meaning of charm is attentiveness, and if that is in fact what charm is, Mr. Astaire was the epitome of it. Fred was just . . . "What's happening? What's going on? Have you seen the new exhibit at the Met?" It was wonderful, having him as one of your parents' friends and then becoming friends with him on an adult level.

Ava Astaire

My stepchildren were very young when their mother died, and I brought them up and always considered them my own. Daddy was marvelous about that. Freddie's three were his only grandchildren actually related to him by blood, but he regarded Pete's and my children as his grandchildren too, and was in contact with all of them.

Below and opposite:
With Fred Junior.

THE ENGLISH

From the time Fred and Adele Astaire first appeared on the stage in London in 1922, they both showed a clear predilection for the English and their way of life. Adele married an English lord, and Fred made many lasting British friendships, which stretched from the racing world in Newmarket to English theatrical figures like Noël Coward and Twiggy to assorted members of the royal family.

In London during the making of *The Midas Run*, 1969.

Outside the Hatchards bookshop during the making of *The Midas Run*, 1969.

Queen Elizabeth, the Queen Mother

Both the King and I were great admirers of Fred Astaire's wonderful talent, and much appreciated his delightful personality.

Hermes Pan

Fred taught the Prince of Wales to dance.

Ava Astaire

I think he *loved* his years in London. He said that the English were mad, all mad.

Lady Alexandra Metcalfe

I first met Fred and Adele in 1923. One evening I was with the Prince of Wales, and we went to see *Stop Flirting* at the Queen's Theatre. It was the second time the Prince of Wales had seen the show, and he sent his equerry, "Fruity" Metcalfe, who later became my husband, backstage between acts to say that the Prince of Wales and his party would like them to join us for dinner at the Riviera Club.

Fruity and Fred and I went out very often in the evening, to many nightclubs, and one saw him at all the parties he was asked to. There was a charming nightclub on the Thames, opposite Dolphin Square. Then there was that nightclub in Grafton Street, where the Medici Gallery is now. It was the first time that Paul Whiteman had come over, and the place was packed. The Prince of Wales, Prince Bertie, Prince Henry, and Prince George—that's it!—they were all there. It shut down at something like one o'clock. Fred loved it there.

Who were all his English friends? Well, I suppose they were all our world, the circle in which we all moved—Edwina Mountbattan, Sheila Loughborough, Paula Casamori. That was his age group, and that was the world that went to parties, and from nightclub to nightclub, and then away for weekends. One always went away from Friday to Monday to some delicious country house nearby. We came back from India, where my father was viceroy, in 1926, so it would have been between 1926 and 1929 that Fred would come and stay with us in the country.

H.R.H. Princess Alexandra

I last saw Fred Astaire in 1979, in the Beverly Wilshire Hotel. He came round one morning and we talked about the past. My mother, Princess Marina, used to tell me a lot about him, and I think he and my father, Prince George, were on Christian-name terms. My father certainly called him Fred.

Bill Self

When Queen Elizabeth visited here, there were some parties which were impossible to get into. I mentioned her visit to Fred, and he said he was seeing her that night. And then he said, "I know her family so well."

Jeremy Tree

He stayed with me the last time he was in England. We went racing at Ascot. Three or four days before, the Queen Mother, who quite often asked me to lunch on that Saturday, got her young equerry to ring me up and ask me to lunch. I told him I had Mr. Fred Astaire staying with me, so sadly I wouldn't be able to. About fifteen minutes later he rang back and said that the Queen Mother was expecting me and Fred Astaire to lunch at Royal Lodge. Fred was a bit horrified at first, but we went to Royal Lodge, and he loved it. He sat between the two queens, because the Queen came to lunch that day. They both made a tremendous fuss of him, and he really enjoyed himself. And then we went and spent the afternoon in the Royal Box at Ascot. He had a lovely time.

Richard McKenzie

When Fred told us about the lunch at Royal Lodge, he said it wasn't as bad as he'd thought it was going to be. He said he relaxed, and that "the little queen was there too."

Letter from H.R.H. The Duke of Kent, Prince George, to Phyllis Astaire. Princess Alexandra had just been born to Prince George and Princess Marina.

Letter from Prince George to Phyllis Astaire on the occasion of his engagement to Princess Marina.

HIS LIKES AND DISLIKES

While making *You'll Never Get Rich*, Fred had a putting green installed outside his bungalow dressing room at Columbia Studios.

Playing miniature golf with Mrs. Hortense Lowits on the roof of the Hotel White, New York.

Fred Astaire was clear and consistent about what he liked and disliked, and his friends could usually predict with fair certainty what his reaction would be to unfamiliar people and things the first time he encountered them. He hated pretentious people and all forms of conspicuous consumption, and he would go to any lengths to avoid them. On the other hand, he was unabashed in the pleasure he got out of the simplest things in life, from homemade soup to his favorite soap opera, "The Guiding Light."

He played with a handicap in the low seventies, 1938.

Ava Astaire

Daddy was a Republican, but politics didn't really grip him. He was very simple about food. He loved meat loaf. Like all Astaires, he couldn't have too much on his plate; if he did, he wouldn't eat anything. Nouvelle cuisine was invented for Daddy, except that he hated the flowers and blueberries.

Bill Self

He loved Chinese food and Italian food. He hated French restaurants, even though the Bistro, his favorite restaurant, was one. He hated the need to deal with the maître d', the captain, etc.

Carol Lynley

He didn't like to eat, and he was not a fancy eater. We used to go to the Bistro, to Chasen's, and to Petrone's on La Cienega (it isn't there anymore), and I used to take him to Dominique's. He liked the food there, but he always said it was too dark. When we went to Chasen's, he would have chicken pot pie; when we went to the Bistro, he also had chicken pot pie. He liked apple sauce. He just wasn't an eater. At the end of his life he stopped eating. He didn't give up; he just wasn't interested. He had no appetite.

Jo Cody

Mr. A. didn't like tomato in his soup. He liked chocolate and vanilla ice cream, but not a lot of it. I think the man just ate to keep alive. Some people live to eat, but that wasn't the case with him.

Sam Goldwyn, Jr.

He went every Sunday to the Episcopal church in Beverly Hills.

Ava Astaire

Daddy was religious. I don't think Mummy went to church much, but after she died Daddy would go with my grandmother. He would sneak out before the end, so he wouldn't have to shake hands. George Roosevelt, a great-nephew or maybe nephew of Franklin Roosevelt, was one of the servers and a very good friend of Daddy's. Daddy loved to go to church when George was taking the collection. He would attach a piece of string to the dollar bill he was donating, and he'd pull it off the collection plate as George stepped away. Daddy was a tease—a little naughty sometimes.

Playing tennis in the 1970s, at the Bel Air home of Peggy and Bill Self.

Mrs. Bill Self

Fred didn't like attending functions. When our son was married, he attended the wedding at St. Alban's Church, much to our surprise. Some years later, our daughter was married in Denver, because her husband was stationed there during the Vietnam War. Bill in passing mentioned to Fred that Barbara was getting married in Denver, and Fred was stricken. He said, "Oh, I don't have to go, do I?"

I wanted Fred to sign some copies of Bob Thomas's book *Astaire*. Bill put some in the car and took them up to Fred's, but we didn't take them in. One of the first things Fred said to me was, "This damn book—everybody wants me to sign one, and I'm fed up with it." So I took him some fudge and told him it was a bribe, because I was going to ask him to do something. The next time I took him some cookies, and I still didn't tell him what it was all about. Finally he couldn't stand it anymore. He called up Bill and asked him what it was that I was going to ask him to do. I'm sure he thought that we wanted him to go to some social function. When Bill told him that I was going to ask him to sign some books, he was filled with relief.

Audrey Hepburn

I remember he used to love playing drums. He had a whole percussion set in his dressing room.

Alfred Vanderbilt

I have no idea if Fred ever read a book. He liked to play pool. I gave him a record once, a record of Alec Wilder songs, and he hated it. He said to me, "It doesn't have a beat, and if music doesn't have a beat I don't want to hear it."

Mrs. Sammy Davis, Jr.

Fred was always so stylish, even playing pool. Sammy does an imitation of him playing pool.

Herb Ross

I went to Fred's home, and he made Bacardis. He showed all his skills at the snooker table; he was an absolutely wonderful pool player.

Carol Lynley

Fred used to play golf with Rita Hayworth. He said she was a very good golfer, which, coming from Fred, was a very big compliment.

Strolling around Beverly Hills.

169

Jack Lemmon

He ceased, in a way, to enjoy things as much when he
would begin, out of age or whatever, not to do them as
well. Two things struck me this way: One was shooting
pool and the other was playing golf. He belonged to the
Bel Air Country Club, and he was a pretty good golfer. He
didn't enjoy not making the good shots that he used to
make, so the fun went out of it, because he was such a
perfectionist. I never played golf then, but we did play a lot
of pool together. Now, I'm a pretty good pool player, but
the reason that Fred could beat me absolutely consistently
was not that he could sink more balls, or that he made
better shots; it was because it was just impossible for me to
watch the man's form and grace—the way he held that cue
and stroked the ball—without being damned intimidated.
He would beat my prat off, every single time. Even though
I knew I could have beaten guys that came close to beating
him. I would just look at his form and think, My God, I
wish we had a camera on this. It was like when he
danced—it was just so beautiful, and fluid, and artistic, and
perfect. About a year before he passed along, I asked him
whether he'd played any pool lately, and he said, "Oh no,
no, can't do it anymore." And it was the same with golf.

Ava Astaire

He didn't like opera at all, or ballet. He really admired
athletes, which had a lot to do with his initial feeling for
Robyn, I think. Daddy loved to play golf, although he
didn't play all that frequently in the later years. When he
broke his wrist skateboarding in 1979, he said that the
break stiffened it and made his golf swing better. He hated
exercise and never took any unless he had to get into shape
for a film.

Carol Lynley

One day, before going out to dinner, he brought out this
piece of paper from Misha Baryshnikov, which he knew I
would be interested in because I love ballet—he never liked
ballet. It was written in a newly formed version of English,
something like "Mr. Astaire, I love you, you are my
favorite, I want to meet you sometime, hopefully, ever
yours, Baryshnikov." Margot Fonteyn showed up once to
meet him.

Douglas Fairbanks, Jr.

He was very shy, and much preferred the company of men.

**Fitting in some photography during
the shooting of *Funny Face*, Paris,
1956.**

Ava Astaire

Daddy drank old-fashioneds. He really enjoyed cocktails. He didn't like wine, but he did like Dom Pérignon. He loved gin rummy. He would play every Sunday afternoon with his best friend, Bill Self. And he loved pool. He really enjoyed backgammon; he and Aunt Dellie learned it from a stagehand. He loved the game shows on television, and he used to like soap operas. He and Jo, the housekeeper, and Aunt Dellie in Phoenix would all watch them and then talk on the telephone for hours about the episodes.

Carol Lynley

Fred would call up and say, "Let's go out and get drunk." And I'd say, "Oh, all right." Not that Fred ever got drunk—he enjoyed cocktails. Then he'd say, "Let's make it two weeks from Thursday," and we'd go to the Bistro. I would drink white wine, and he'd have old-fashioneds. He loved those very thirties cocktails.

Bill Self

He loved baseball, but didn't like football.

Ava Astaire

He was fascinated by things that were slightly off. Once he was with Jock Whitney, or one of that group, and they went to a brothel in Paris. He wouldn't partake—he sat down and waited for them—but he loved the whole atmosphere. Daddy loved making *The Towering Inferno* because he could have water poured all over him. He loved how it left him disheveled, which was not the usual image of him. People would ask him about the old movies, and he just genuinely wasn't interested. And he didn't read at all.

Playing backgammon, 1935.

Practicing on his drums.

Jack Haley, Jr.

It's probably three or four months before the release of *That's Entertainment*. Everybody has done their piece, and it's time for the kick-off announcing the picture. Liza and I go and pick up Fred, and then Gene Kelly, and the four of us are in the limo. It's ten-thirty in the morning, and we're on our way to Metro. They are going in front of the press and are having to think of what they are going to say. Sammy Davis is meeting us there. Fred is whining about hating this kind of stuff, about how he thought all this was over in his life, and was it for a good cause? "Yes," I said, "the money will be going to the motion-picture fund." It's a long ride from here to Culver City. Halfway there, there's a lull in the conversation, and Fred turns to me and says, "Jack, I've been watching some of the foreign pictures. Have you seen any of those nominated this year? Gene, did you see *Turkish Delight?* It's a very interesting picture." It was the first X-rated picture to be nominated for an Oscar.

Fred liked to sneak down to the Pussy Cat Theater. he would wait for a gloomy day, and he'd put on his hat and sunglasses and sneak into these porno movies.

Bill Self

He watched the soap operas, and he would ask me about them, because he knew I worked at CBS. He would ask me what was going to happen next, or, if he couldn't watch on a certain day, he would ask me what he had missed in the plot. He was most surprised when I told him that I didn't watch them.

Patricia Prior

Fred and Adele both had a passion for the soap operas; his favorite was "The Guiding Light" and hers was "As the World Turns." They loved the theater element in the soap operas. They couldn't believe that these actors played their part day in and day out.

Mrs. Jock Whitney

In the years that we were friends, Fred visited us in Georgia to shoot quail, which, I must admit, was not his best sport. He and Jock used to play a lot of golf together.

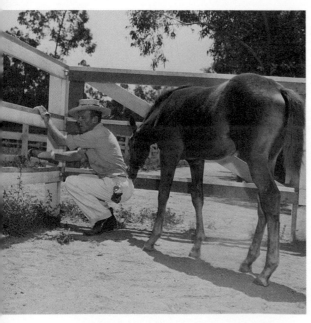

Repairing a fence at his ranch, Chatsworth, 1952.

Jamie Niven

Daddy and Fred used to go fishing together a lot, and they used to go to the track a lot. They fished from Catalina Island; they used to rent a boat down in San Pedro, and off they'd go. They both wore gray flannels for their fishing expeditions, not blue jeans. I don't think Fred owned a pair of blue jeans. Daddy didn't. I'll always remember them, both in their gray flannels, setting off in Fred's extraordinarily highly tuned Cadillac, heading for San Pedro to get on their boat.

Bill Self

At one time we were both into cars. When Mrs. Bull, Phyllis's aunt, died, Fred was the executor of the estate, which included a Rolls Royce. Fred had a Rolls, so he said he would sell that one to me for $10,000, which was very little, but my wife said she would be embarrassed to go and buy a pint of milk in a Rolls Royce. Fred later had a Maserati, but he didn't like it, so he didn't keep it for long.

Dr. Harry Reizner

He had a large garage, and he'd always show my wife and me his Rolls Royce. He really cherished that car. It was always polished. He'd even go out and do it himself. Often, when I'd arrive, he'd be out there shining away.

Carol Lynley

He took up skateboarding late in life, and broke his wrist. One day he rang me and told me excitedly to come on up, because he had a new thing. He'd seen his grandchild on a skateboard, and had become enamored of it.

Dr. Harry Reizner

When he did that picture with the Dobermans, *The Amazing Dobermans*, he was scared stiff. He liked horses, but he was wary about dogs, especially since these dogs are trained to be ferocious.

Ava Astaire

Animals loved Daddy. We had a cat that Kim Novak gave him called Carlye—it was named after the character Kim played with him in *The Notorious Landlady*—but it got eaten by coyotes. Then there was a dog of mine, Allison, which stayed behind when I got married. Animals came to him. The dog in *Purple Taxi* didn't take to anybody except his trainer, but the first day of shooting he went straight over to Daddy. He loved Daddy.

Fred Astaire won the Capistrano Handicap at Santa Anita Racetrack and received the Gold Cup from Lee Batson, president of the Santa Anita Turf Club; with jockey Jay Jessop and trainer Clyde Philips.

xcept for work and family, racing was the consuming passion of Fred Astaire's life. He got the taste for it in England in the 1920s. He went to the races all his life and developed his own special betting systems. He eventually owned a string of racehorses, and had three horses named after him by his friends. His first wife came from a prominent East Coast racing family, and his second wife was a professional jockey.

Mrs. Fred Astaire, Jr., Ava, Fred, and Fred Junior, 1958.

Jeremy Tree

Fred loved Saratoga. I met Fred with Jock Whitney, whose horses I trained. I think Fred first got involved with racing way back when he and Adele were in London. He had some great friends called Leach, a jockey and a trainer, in Newmarket, back in the late twenties, early thirties.

Slim Keith

Jock Whitney called his last great horse Fred Astaire.

Alfred Vanderbilt

Fred loved horses. I once had a butler who'd been with me from the time I was twenty-one. He loved the horses, too, and he and the man who was training horses for me at that time pooled their money and bought a racehorse, which did pretty well. Fred was at dinner one night, and when Louis, my butler, came around the table and passed the meat to Fred, Fred said, "Do you want to sell that horse, Louis?" Next time Louis came round, Louis said, "Yes, Mr. Astaire. What do you think he's worth?" And this went on, back and forth, for the whole meal.

Fred had a good horse called Triplicate, which was not a super horse, but it won a lot of races. I don't think Fred ever had more than three or four at one time. He had a horse that did well in England, called Rainbow Tie. Then he bought a horse from Jock, and then he bought a horse from me, called Early Bird.

Lester Holt

I was Mr. Astaire's trainer for twenty years or more. I once took one of his horses up to San Francisco to race, and from then on we were associated. He loved racing. It is one of those things that gets to you. He loved the horses. We'd always sit together at the track. He would bet, but only for fun. He had his own systems for betting, but I don't think they worked; he'd count up and down, and he'd use the alphabet. In all our years, we never had a cross word between us. He was very good at imitating, and whenever I'd leave the box he'd do me. He'd always wear a silk scarf like a kerchief. He never bothered me about the horses. I asked him a question once, and he said, "That's your department." That's why we got along so good, I guess.

With his horse Triplicate, 1949.

Mrs. Lester Holt

He liked systems to bet the horses. I was up in northern California during part of a Santa Anita meeting, and Fred sent me the racing forms from the previous day. He'd circled the horses that he'd bet on and that had won on his system. He didn't bet very much money; he was having fun. They were always long prices, no short-price horses at all, and this one day there were three or four in a block. He made up his system just to amuse himself. Why did Fred love the races and horses? Well, he was from the Midwest, and I think people from there are very close to animals and close to the soil. So I think it was more an inborn love of animals. I can't think of a soul in the racing world that didn't adore Fred. He was a gentle man. Fred didn't intrude at the stable during working hours, but he'd come down to the paddock on racing days. Until Danny, his chauffeur, died, they'd always come to the races together. Danny had been a taxi driver in New York. Bing Crosby used to come racing quite a lot, and Fred and Bing were very close friends. Bill Winfrey was Fred's trainer before Lester. Fred and Robyn never came racing together after they were married.

Bill Winfrey

I met Fred Astaire in the fifties, when he came to California. I met him with Alfred Vanderbilt. Fred Astaire had just got into racing. I think it started for him in England. It was less commercial and more sporty then. He loved sport. He knew a lot about racing. He would study the forms. He had his own way of betting, his own system. He would look down the list of horses alphabetically and stop on certain letters. I never understood it, but it seemed to work, and he won on many outsiders.

Molly Keane

Fred loved Newmarket. There were two brothers there who were his great friends, the Leach brothers. Whenever he was staying at Lismore, he always went over to Newmarket to see Jack Leach.

He used to go to race meetings with Charlie, Dellie's husband. With Charlie and Charlie's two guardians, rather, because Charlie was inclined to get a bit boozed up at the meetings. His guardians were Russell, the butler, and Paddy, the undertaker, who owned some good horses. And do you know, the extraordinary thing is that Paddy, the undertaker, had a coffin which he kept up in his loft, and it was frightfully grand. It was called a silver casket, and Charlie booked it for himself. A dreadful casket—you can imagine what it was like!

With his horse Over Anxious, 1949.

With David Niven at the Santa Anita Racetrack, March 1937.

With Robert Montgomery at the Riviera Country Club, February 1935.

At the races with Hermes Pan and Phyllis, in the 1930s.

The Duke of Devonshire

I can remember the first time I met Fred Astaire as if it were yesterday. Adele and her husband, Uncle Charlie, took my father and me to see *Gay Divorcee,* and we went backstage afterwards. It was the first time I'd ever been behind, and I had this marvelous bit of luck, because Fred, as you know, adored horse racing, and he happened to mention it, and to my great good fortune I had the form book in my coat pocket, so I produced it. From that moment onwards we were firm friends. That was in the early thirties.

What Fred liked to do when he was visiting at Lismore was walk up a quarter of a mile from the house to Lismore village, go to the grocery shop called the Winevaults, run into a charming man called Mr. McCarthy, and then go on to the betting shop. His morning routine. He always wore dark spectacles, hoping that people wouldn't recognize him. I shall always remember this very dapper figure with his dark glasses walking up to the betting shop at Lismore, looking in fact very conspicuous on the main street of the village. He used to enjoy a bet in a totally harmless way.

He had one or two horses in England, but I don't think they ever did much good. He was staying at Lismore when my very good mare won the very big Ascot race, and the first telegram I got was from him.

Peter Duchin

I spent two or three weekends with him at the Whitneys' house in the fifties and sixties. He loved horse racing and he loved the Whitneys, and they loved him. I would try to time my visits to Saratoga for when he was there, because it was such fun to be with him. He was kind of shy, but in that ambience he felt very alive, and it was clear that he really enjoyed the very highfalutin life. He didn't mind at all being pampered, waited on, rubbed. He liked the adulation, the praise. During those weekends he'd get up early, watch the horses train, go to the track. He'd swim in the afternoon, and then there'd be a dinner party.

Whitney Tower

I imagine Fred liked racing for the graceful movement of the horses. He also liked the competition, and the association with other people who liked horses. There's a camaraderie involved in racing that is very hard to describe, yet it's there. It doesn't really exist in other sports.

Howard W. Koch
I met Fred years ago in Saratoga Springs, about 1934 or 1935. My father was a bookmaker, and Fred was one of his customers.

Jimmy Kilroe
I first met Fred out here at the Santa Anita racetrack. He was very self-effacing. He would come out here to this track at least once a week. After Danny, his chauffeur, died, he would come alone on the whole. I suspect he got the taste for racing back East, because Jock Whitney, who was one of his best friends, had a large stable. So did Jock's sister, Joan Payson.

Ava Astaire
He loved racing. He first got the bug in England. Mummy loved it, too. Her uncle was Henry Bull, so she was brought up in the atmosphere of Belmont. All the needlework rugs in our house in Ireland were done by Mummy between races at Hollywood Park. Daddy had a very good horse called Rainbow Tie. Then, of course, there was Triplicate. The last race I ever went to with him was the Breeders' Cup, in November 1986. Daddy had to go to that race because a horse was named after him by Betsy Whitney. It was called Fred Astaire. He had three horses named after him.

Alfred Vanderbilt
Years ago, in the thirties, I named a horse after Fred, and he was out of a mare called Night and Day. I named the horse Fred Astaire, and Fred was terribly flattered. Then I had to geld him. He was a bad horse. About 1985, Betsy named a horse Fred Astaire, and he was a pretty good horse. Later, Fred said to me, "I'm sick of all these goddamn people naming horses after me, and asking whether that's okay with me *afterwards*," and I said, "Fred, you've had in your life two horses named after you that I know of—one by me fifty years ago and this one now. Come off it."

Fred and Phyllis Astaire at the Santa Anita Racetrack.

Stanley Donen
I used to see Fred at the races when I went with Cary Grant, who was a close, close friend of mine. The last time I saw Fred, he was having lunch at Hollywood Park racetrack, about six months before he died. He was frail. He had an inner-ear problem which affected his balance.

HIS CHARACTER

Yes, *Fred had a sense of humor, a very special one. And yes, he could be grumpy when the occasion provoked him. But mainly his friends remember him as a sweet, shy, loyal person, an enduring combination of Omaha, Hollywood, Oyster Bay, and St. James's.*

Cyd Charisse

When you worked with him he was a gentleman, and in private he was a gentleman. In public he was a very humble, sweet man, a marvelous person.

Jamie Niven

Fred was revered, a sort of Charles Boyer–type figure. You didn't tease Fred; you treated him with the greatest respect. I always remember him being very considerate towards younger people. He had time for you. But it was my father's reaction to him that always struck me most. He was different with Fred than with anyone else, except for Charles. It must have been because he really thought they were terrific people. Fred had style, class. Daddy was much less likely with him to tease, to be loud, to tell off-color stories, which he told a lot of. My father had quite bad language in private—we had to take four hundred four-letter words out of the first book. But he never told jokes with punch lines which had rough words in front of Fred.

Hermes Pan

Fred had a very odd sense of humor, which is hard to explain. He had a pixie sense of humor. He never gossiped about people.

Lily Guest

Fred had a shy, nice sense of humor. Things would suddenly strike him as being funny, and he would laugh— that's a sense of humor.

Leslie Caron

You could kid around with him. He chit-chatted. He was very natural and gossipy. He used to tell us how Judy Garland was overeating, and how it was no wonder she became so huge. He'd say, "We'd have one ice cream and she'd have four. We'd have one hot dog and she'd have three." He had a great sense of humor.

Jean Howard

Once you brought him out, he told wonderful stories. His humor wasn't joke humor—no jokes per se.

Liza Minnelli

Fred was witty in his own quiet way. He had a point of view that was funny. Things that people did in real life struck him funny, as opposed to jokes.

Lady Alexandra Metcalfe

He really was a most unconceited man and totally unaware of being the star he was. He had no airs whatsoever. Never expected to be recognized. And he was shy about being recognized if he walked into a restaurant. That was Fred's character.

Leslie Caron

He was worried about whether the public would accept the age gap between us—I was twenty-three and he was fifty-five. He coped with this intelligently. He used his sense of humor. He was so tactful, like when he would ask me about my dress for such and such a scene. He always referred to the famous Ginger feather-dress scene, in *Top Hat,* when the feathers got in his mouth and up his nostrils.

Carol Lynley

He had a fabulous wry sense of humor, very Irish, almost black Irish. He could make a joke out of the most terrible things, and he could make something terrible out of something wonderful. One day we were talking about something he was doing with Helen Hayes—they were shooting together—and he said, "Oh, Helen, she's so . . . she's so sweet."

His humor must never be underestimated. I'll give you an example of Fred's humor. At Christmas, he usually sent me Dom Pérignon, but a couple of years in a row he sent me some very narrow cylinders, and inside were plastic Christmas trees. When you plugged them in, the lights lit up. When I thanked him for these, he answered that he was just trying to make it easier for me. (I really don't like Christmas.) He was mentally elegant, with a choice of verbiage, a sense of humor, and a point of view that were truly and originally elegant.

Roddy McDowall

He used to make me scream with laughter. It wasn't his timing, it was his view.

Audrey Hepburn

I never saw him cross, never. Maybe he has been, or he was at home, I don't know; but I never saw him, ever. I've never even heard he was difficult.

Stanley Donen

He was often crotchety. Oh yes. In *Funny Face,* there was a dance number outside, and I wanted a lot of white doves walking around on the ground. So I put the doves there, and he knew they were going to be there, but when it came to doing it he was worried. He was dancing, and he wanted it to be good. Sometimes there'd be a take where the doves would be in the way. I'd clipped their wings slightly so they wouldn't fly away, but they would wander away. Anyway, he was trying to do his best under trying circumstances, but those doves did bother him. Finally he yelled, "I don't want them here! Get those ducks out of the way! Those ducks are in my way! Get rid of those ducks!" This same sequence was done outside on grass, between two little streams, in France. It was raining terribly, and it rained for weeks and weeks. Finally it stopped, so we went out to shoot on this little island. But the grass was ankle deep in bog. Audrey had on little heels, and they kept swishing into the mud. He got very scruffy and said to me, "I can't dance in that. Fix it." I told him we'd do what we could, but how could we fix it? He said, "I don't care! Put down wood and paint it green."

Irving "Swifty" Lazar

He was an enchanting man when he felt like it, and when he didn't he was not. He was very aloof, very distant. He could be quite irascible and difficult. The only person who I think ever reached him, whom he really liked, was Hermes Pan.

David Bailey

He was a bit grumpy when I photographed him—I don't know why, maybe he didn't want to be photographed. It was the same thing when I photographed Laurence Olivier; they're such myths that you don't believe they're real. Anyway, Fred cheered up when his daughter came in.

Douglas Fairbanks, Jr.

He could be pretty crabby. One day in Beverly Hills, I was on my way back from using my father's pool and I dropped in on Fred. After I'd been there a short time, a group of Fred's acquaintances called by unexpectedly. He was so sharp with them that they left very soon after arriving.

Anthony Perkins

He would tell you so much, and then he would stop. In his book, *Steps in Time,* for instance, that's the way he deals with his first wife's death; he goes so far and then he stops. And the next thing you know, the next chapter starts off brightly as if nothing had happened. And that was very illustrative of how he was in real life as well.

Ava Astaire

He only lost his temper if something interfered with his work. Or if someone was nasty to me, he'd go through the roof.

Leslie Caron

In a very sweet way, he would insist on perfection. He could be angry and crabby if anything went wrong. For instance, he once stepped on my foot during a number and he yelled at me. I yelled right back at him.

The Duke of Devonshire

He had great charm, but, to be slightly unkind, he wasn't frightfully interesting. But, then, why should he have been?

Eleanor Lambert

He was just so easy. He never behaved badly toward people he didn't like; he just avoided them.

Whitney Tower

There was a handful of people that you could put into one category, as real, first-class gents: Jimmy Stewart, Cary Grant, Fred Astaire.

Irving "Swifty" Lazar

Fred Astaire gave the impression that he was a highbrow, but he was not. He came from a small town in Nebraska. He picked up a little polish working in England and getting to Paris, but he was never what I would call a very sophisticated or debonair fellow at all. No mind for small talk. He was a perfectly nice man, but he was not a high-style English gentleman. He was nothing like that. He was Omaha.

Roddy McDowall

The public reacts to certain people, like Fred Astaire and Myrna Loy, with great deference. They set a tone in a room, they set an atmosphere. You wouldn't think of being vulgar with Fred. You'd be on your best behavior. There was a muted joy about him, but you'd never think of rushing up to him and being effusive. There was something royal about him.

What woman hasn't dreamed of dancing with Fred Astaire? A number of those who had the dream come true report that the world's greatest dancer had two left feet when it came to getting up and dancing at a party. However, the thrill of being whisked anywhere in those arms more than compensated.

Dancing with the Empress Farah Diba of Iran at a party at the White House.

Douglas Fairbanks, Jr.

I always heard from the girls that he was not such a hot dance partner at parties.

Nancy Reagan

My husband and I once gave a dinner for Princess Alexandra and Angus Ogilvie, and knowing that Fred was a good friend of theirs, I asked him to come. I really didn't expect him to, because he rarely went out socially, especially to a fairly large party. As we sat at the table, it became obvious no one was going to dance until we did. I turned to Fred and said, "I need your help. No one will dance until we do, so would you just go around the floor once with me to get everyone started?" Well, once around the floor with Fred Astaire was an unforgettable experience. I was sure I looked like Ginger Rogers!

H.R.H. Princess Alexandra

When Ronald Reagan was governor of California, he and his wife gave a party in Los Angeles, in 1970 or 1972, and I danced with Fred. It was very funny, because my dear husband meanly hoped that I might fall down, which I didn't. Fred danced rather self-consciously, rather formally, which I remember surprised me slightly.

Rocky Converse

All my life I hoped that he would ask me to dance, because I was a pretty good dancer, if I say it myself. So came the night. It was a big, big disaster. I think Fred needed people who had a routine and knew the routine. Of course, I thought it was me until I talked to another girl who'd had my experience, and she said, "Oh God, he's the worst dancer I've met in my life." Ballroom dancer, that is. With me it was disastrous; it was just zilch. I think we tried it twice, but not thrice.

Lady Alexandra Metcalfe

Did I ever dance with him? Oh yes, often, but he just shuffled around—he was no excitement to dance with. All the other people like Jock Whitney were far, far better dancers. When you danced with Fred, he did the minimum, and so you were quite unaware of the fact—thank God!—of who he was. Thank God, because you might have been unable to do what he would have wanted you to do. He was a very, very quiet dancer.

Slim Keith

One night I was at a party, a Hollywood tent party, and Fred came over and asked me to dance. I stood up so flattered and terrified that when the music started he was holding on to Lot's wife; I'd become a pillar of salt. I said, "Thank you very much, Fred, but I'm too scared," and he sat me down.

Betty Comden

We'd occasionally see him at a big social event. I remember seeing him at one party of Lauren Bacall's, and I thought, Wouldn't it be wonderful to dance with Fred Astaire? But he doesn't like to ballroom dance. My husband went over and asked Fred if he would dance with me, and he did. I thought he was wonderful, but he explained to me that he never liked social dancing. We did a very sedate fox-trot.

Ava Astaire

He would be awkward at parties, because he knew he was being watched. When I came out in '59, and fathers and daughters waltzed, we were the only ones that went the wrong way around the room. We just did it all wrong.

Stanley Donen

I remember Fred once said to me, when Ava was still in school, "I don't like going to school functions, but I go because I want her to know I care. It's very difficult, though, because there are balls, and all the fathers get up and dance with their daughters. When I would get up to dance with Ava, the floor would part and everybody would look at us, so I ceased to be just somebody with his daughter."

Emma Soames

When I was living in Paris in the early seventies, my father was the British ambassador, and I used to spend probably more time than was good for me in an outfit called New Jimmy's, Le New Jimmy's, on the Boulevard Raspail. It was owned by an elegant creature of the night called Régine. There were two hot spots in Paris then: one was Jimmy's, which was yuppie, and the other one was real decadence—Castel's. Anyway, one night in New Jimmy's I found myself sitting at a table with, among other people, Fred Astaire, and he asked me to dance. It was smoochy stuff. I remember thinking at the time, "Hello, could this be one for the memoirs?" He danced like a dream. I even managed not to trip up over him, but that's the sign of a really good dancer, that you never do trip up. He then armed me back to the table, where I attracted a gratifying number of envious looks.

Liza Minnelli

When I was about seventeen, I danced with him at a party. It was a rock 'n' roll song, with heavy drums, and he was dancing away, and then he looked at me and said, "I always tried to get this sound on the drums at Metro." He wanted the best really laid down.

Mrs. Sammy Davis, Jr.

Fred came here for my big eighties party, and also to Sammy's fiftieth, when I had everybody dress up like children. It was a nice surprise, and I put all the baby pictures around. George Burns wore tap shoes. Somebody came with a pogo stick. Everybody thought Fred would come in his tap shoes, but he wore little slippers. Bedroom slippers.

Ginger Rogers

Yes, I danced with him socially. It was at a big party which David Selznick and his wife gave. He was there with his wife, and there was no way for him to keep from dancing with me. And the whole room stopped dead to watch us.

David Niven, Jr.

There was this huge luncheon at MGM after the movie *That's Dancing*, which I produced, and Fred sat next to me and we talked about Daddy. Fred told me that the one thing he really felt he'd failed at in life was being able to teach my father to do anything more than just the box step in a fox-trot. He was constantly trying to teach Daddy to do rumbas and congas and tangos and sambas and cha-chas, but Daddy couldn't do a thing. He was very happy with a box step. He wouldn't even go forward; it was just the box step. So Fred said that his great failure was not teaching David at least one more step.

Mrs. Jock Whitney

One night when Fred was staying with us in Manhasset, Jock asked Fred to help him perfect the new dance, the Sluefoot. The next morning, Fred complained of having spent a sleepless night due to the fact that Jock had practiced the Sluefoot all night long in his bedroom, which was directly over Fred's room.

Jeremy Tree

We had one lovely evening at Saratoga, not long before Jock died. We came back to Jock's house at about eleven-thirty, after the evening sales, and Peter Duchin, who was staying, sat down at the piano and started playing a lot of the old Astaire tunes, and Fred started singing. We had a great time, and the evening ended up with Fred and Jock dancing the Black Bottom together.

Peter Duchin

He was really easy to play for, on that well-remembered night. He knew what he was doing, and he remembered all the words. And he'd remember stories about the songs. He wasn't giggly. He was obviously animated by work; that was clear the moment he started singing.

I loved the reaction of Joan Payson, Jock Whitney's sister, the day after that great evening in Saratoga. "You shit!" she called across to us as we were sitting in our racing box. This huge mountain of a woman. "What, Joan?" I yelled back. "You didn't call and wake me up and tell me to come over."

Showing an instructor at the Fred Astaire Dance Studio how to do the Astaire, a ballroom swing trot Fred created.

FINALE

The eight-year-old Fred Astaire, 1907.

Fred danced for the last time professionally in 1976 at the age of seventy-seven. He last acted in a dramatic film in 1981. He died of pneumonia on June 22, 1987. He had just turned eighty-eight. But the films and his legend are here to stay.

Having a laugh, 1959.

Frank Sinatra
I only have one thing to say about Fred: He could have been the classiest performer I have ever known in all my years in show business.

Audrey Hepburn
Talk of unique, talk of a legend—I wonder if he ever realized how big he was. I think he knew that he'd made it, and that he was damned good at his job, and a big, big star. You can't not realize that.

Betty Comden
There was never anybody like him.

Nancy Reagan
A true legend. There will never be another like him.

Leslie Caron
I think the greatest compliment you can pay anyone who had such a glorious career in Hollywood is to say that he was normal. I last saw Fred at a tribute for Gene Kelly. It was a big ball at the Hilton in Hollywood. Fred and I were standing near a staircase, and a waiter going up brushed against me and threw me off balance. As quick as a flash, Fred, who was eighty-five, grabbed my wrist and steadied me. I said, "Fred, you haven't lost your grip."

Roddy McDowall
One can be perfectly mannered in the living room and a son of a bitch in the arena, but he was tremendously gracious in relation to everything that he did.

Ava Astaire
Only in the last years did I telephone him more than he telephoned me, because the long-distance dialing got a little confusing for him. After Richard and I left California the last time, I became terrified of sleeping near the telephone. About two weeks before Daddy went into hospital, the telephone rang at two o'clock in the morning. We thought, Oh God, this is it. But it was Daddy himself, calling us in the strongest voice. He said he realized he'd made a mistake about the time and sent love all around.

Molly Keane
Although I never really had proper subjects in common with Fred, at the same time it was so easy to be with him that I didn't feel like an embarrassed old bog-trotter.

Carol Lynley
Fred was Fred. Fred was a valentine.

Jeremy Tree
The year before he died, I had dinner with him and Ava and Richard in a rather dark French restaurant in Hollywood which he liked very much. And when we got up to leave, everybody clapped.

Jack Haley, Jr.
In 1974 there was a lunch to celebrate *That's Entertainment.* Gene Kelly, David Niven, Jr., and I were there early, at the Club Room at MGM. It was all set at one big table. Nobody else was allowed in. We're sitting there fidgeting, and in come the Nicholas Brothers, and then there's applause and it's Leslie Caron, and then there's more applause and it's Debbie Reynolds, and then Cyd Charisse, and then there's a lull for a moment and people start shouting and it's Fred. The whole building was shouting. After lunch all the dancers went to have their picture taken, and while we were waiting for this, Buddy Ebsen started teaching Fred to moonwalk like Michael Jackson. That was a great sight.

David Niven, Jr.
After the lunch for *That's Entertainment,* we had to go to one of the sound stages to have a big group picture taken, and we walked there. Although I was asked to hurry Fred along, he just meandered, like a rather decrepit, frail old man. Finally I said, "Fred, do you think you could pick up the pace? We have to do this picture at two o'clock, and it's a minute to two. Everybody has to get the fuck out of here. So let's ride in your car"—which was following us at the speed of a wounded snail—"or let's pick up the pace." Fred said, "All right, let's pick up the pace." And he took off like a rocket, suddenly no longer this dithering person. He shouted back, "Is this fast enough for you, David?" as he rushed off at about eighteen steps a second. He told me that people treat you as an old man when you get old, and all one really needs is someone to tell one to move it.

I used to run into him in the flats of Beverly Hills, wearing a hat and glasses, and we used to wander along window-shopping. He'd tell me what a pain in the ass it was to get old. He said that when you get old, the only thing that's guaranteed to go up is your gums.

Roddy McDowall
Fred never waned. He was terrific, but a lot of people who are terrific don't manage to hold an unbroken line until they're seventy-two. And he did quite a few movies after that as an actor!

Ahmet Ertegun

The last time I saw him was when he was honored at the Kennedy Center in 1978. I went down to Washington with Mick Jagger and Jerry Hall and my wife.

Rudolf Nureyev

He did everything. He said everything he had to say. His dance is recorded incredibly well. He's there for eternity.

Carol Lynley

Had he not been Fred Astaire, had he not been the talented genius that he was, had he just been another person with another name, he still had an extraordinary ability to live life as it should be lived. He never gave anybody up. He had a chauffeur for thirty years, and when the chauffeur died, he drove himself. He had this ability to turn every twenty-four hours into a joyful experience, and that's a genius besides his physical genius.

Slim Keith

Billy Wilder's recurrent nightmare—he referred to it as a nightmare, but in fact it's a dream—is that he's walking down Rodeo Drive and looks up and sees Fred, who looks just marvelous. Billy says, "How's everything going, Fred?" "Oh," says Fred, "just fine. I just finished a picture with Ginger, and it's out and it's doing very well. What are you doing, Billy?" "Well, I'm also doing very well, and I've been nominated for an Academy Award." They discuss life generally, and then Billy says, "Fred, you know there's something I've always wanted to ask you, and I've never had the nerve to do it, but I'm going to do it now." Fred says, "Anything. What is it?" And Billy says, "Who's your tailor?" And then Billy always wakes up, before he gets the answer.

With Rita Hayworth, in an advertisement for Chesterfield cigarettes.

Mikhail Baryshnikov

Classical dancers can cope with their legends—Nijinsky did this and that—but it's from books that we know about it, from photographs that don't move. The problem with Astaire is that he's everywhere—moving. You give your own performance, and receive applause, and you think, Maybe, just maybe, it was successful. Then you go home feeling good and turn on the television to relax, and there he is, making you nervous all over again. All the clichés about Mr. Astaire—his elegance, his imagination, his wit, his virtuosity—are so very true, so very real. And we are, of course, very lucky; his gift, captured in the movies, is one we can all share forever. He was, and always will be, our never-ending legend.

Twiggy

One night I went out to dinner with Fred and Hermes Pan. We had a lovely meal in a Malaysian restaurant, wonderful Chinese food and drinks in coconuts, which are always much stronger than you think they're going to be. We all had one of those, and although we weren't drunk, it obviously hit us harder than some people, since none of us drank much usually. Anyway, we had a lovely time, and then we came out of the restaurant and had to walk down the street to Fred's car. It was dark except for the streetlights, and Fred started to dance down the street. He did this incredible tap dance, and he ended in a double turn on his knees with his arms up to the sky and said, "Hollywood, I love you." Afterwards, I always wondered whether people driving up that street must have thought they were dreaming.

Liza Minnelli

The last time I saw Fred was the day my father was buried. Fred came to the house, and he took the time to sit beside me—he was very shaky by that point—and tell me a wonderful story about my dad. My dad was a perfectionist too, and Fred said that when they were working on *The Band Wagon,* on the sequence with the arcade, when the tall lady screams, Vincente would say to this lady, "Do it this way—no, no, do it this way." Finally she said, just into the air, "That man is driving me crazy." There was this silence, because everybody thought that Vincente would get mad. Fred said that he got a little worried, and walked over to a corner to get out of the way. Vincente came over to him and said, "You know, she's right. I do drive everybody crazy." That was a lovely thing to tell me.

Jack Haley, Jr.

There was a memorial service for David Niven here in Hollywood about a month after he died. Cary Grant and I were ushers, and Fred was there. There was a little side entrance, and he and Gregory Peck and Jamie and David Niven were standing there. I walked up to them, and Fred asked me to take his arm. It was awful having to help the most graceful man in the world down a simple flight of steps.

Jamie Niven

My father emceed the American Film Institute tribute to Fred Astaire in 1981. Now, the disease that my father had, had big ups and downs. Daddy opened the tribute by apologizing on national television for his voice, saying that it belonged to a parrot. His clothes didn't fit very well, because he'd lost so much weight; he'd borrowed a dinner jacket from the headwaiter. Fred knew that Daddy was very sick. I don't think anyone else knew, except for us, and he was deeply moved by that.

When my father died, my brother, David, and I organized a memorial service for him in California. This was October 1983, and Fred was not at all well then. He hadn't been seen in public for a long time. He came to the memorial service and sat between David and me, and he said, "I know that your father would have wanted me to sit here. The only sad thing is that the roles should really have been reversed." That was the most touching thing I can remember about Fred.

Carol Lynley

He was fragility and steel.

Sam Goldwyn, Jr.

Nice man, a really nice man. Who else left a testimony of work like that? He is the only one who has ever totally mastered film.

Mrs. Jock Whitney

The last time I saw Fred was at the service for Jock, where he was a pallbearer. I can visualize them both, with the angels, dancing up a storm.

David Bailey's portrait of Fred Astaire, taken in Ireland in 1978.

A FRED ASTAIRE CHRONOLOGY

1897 September 10	Adele Astaire born in Omaha, Nebraska.
1899 May 10	Fred Astaire born in Omaha, Nebraska.
1905	Ann Astaire enters her two children, Fred and Adele, in vaudeville in New York.
1917 November 28	Fred and Adele open in their first New York musical, *Over the Top*, at the Forty-fourth Street Roof.
1918 July 25	*The Passing Show of 1918* opens at the Winter Garden, New York.
1919 October 7	*Apple Blossoms* opens at the Globe, New York.
1921 October 4	*The Love Letter* opens at the Globe, New York.
1922 February 20	*For Goodness Sake* opens at the Lyric, New York.
1923 May 30	*Stop Flirting* opens at the Shaftesbury, London.
1924 December 1	*Lady, Be Good!* opens at the Liberty, New York, with music by George and Ira Gershwin.
1926 April 14	*Lady, Be Good!* opens at the Empire, London.
1927 November 22	*Funny Face* opens at the Alvin, New York, with music by George and Ira Gershwin.
1928 November 8	*Funny Face* opens at Prince's, London.
1930 November 18	*Smiles* opens at the Ziegfeld, New York.
1931 June 3	*The Band Wagon* opens at the New Amsterdam, New York, with music by Howard Dietz and Arthur Schwartz, also starring Tilly Losch.
1932 Summer	Adele Astaire marries Lord Charles Cavendish, younger brother of the Duke of Devonshire, in Ireland, and retires from show business forever.
1932 November 29	*The Gay Divorcée* opens at the Ethel Barrymore, New York, with music by Cole Porter, also starring Claire Luce.
1933 November 2	*The Gay Divorcée* opens at the Palace, London, also starring Claire Luce.
1933 July 12	Fred Astaire marries Phyllis Livingstone Potter and they move to Hollywood.
1933 December 2	Fred Astaire's first movie, *Dancing Lady*, is released, with music by, among others, Arthur Freed, also starring Joan Crawford and Clark Gable.

Fred with his daughter, Ava, in Paris, 1956.

1933 December 20	*Flying Down to Rio*, Fred's first of ten films with Ginger Rogers and first of ten RKO movies, is released, also starring Delores Del Rio.
1934 October 3	*The Gay Divorcée* is released, directed by Mark Sandrich, with music by Cole Porter, also starring Ginger Rogers, Edward Everett Horton, Eric Blore, and Erik Rhodes.
1935 February 13	*Roberta* is released, with music by Oscar Hammerstein and Jerome Kern, also starring Ginger Rogers, Irene Dunne, and Randolph Scott.
1935 September 6	*Top Hat* is released, directed by Mark Sandrich, with music by Irving Berlin, also starring Ginger Rogers, Edward Everett Horton, Helen Broderick, Eric Blore, and Erik Rhodes.
1936 January 21	Fred Astaire, Jr., is born.
1936 February 2	*Follow the Fleet* is released, directed by Mark Sandrich, music by Irving Berlin, also starring Ginger Rogers, Randolph Scott, Lucille Ball, and Betty Grable.
1936 August 26	*Swing Time* is released, directed by George Stevens, music by Dorothy Fields and Jerome Kern, also starring Ginger Rogers, Helen Broderick, Eric Blore, and Betty Furness.
1937 April 30	*Shall We Dance?* is released, directed by Mark Sandrich, with music by George and Ira Gershwin, also starring Ginger Rogers, Helen Broderick, and Betty Furness.
1937 July 11	George Gershwin dies.
1937 November 20	*A Damsel in Distress* is released, directed by George Stevens, music by George and Ira Gershwin, also starring George Burns, Gracie Allen, and Joan Fontaine.
1938 August 30	*Carefree* is released, directed by Mark Sandrich, with music by Irving Berlin, also starring Ginger Rogers and Ralph Bellamy.
1939 March 31	*The Story of Vernon and Irene Castle* is released, also starring Ginger Rogers.
1940 February 14	*Broadway Melody of 1940* is released, with music by Cole Porter, also starring Eleanor Powell and George Murphy.
1940 December 3	*Second Chorus* is released, with music by Johnny Mercer, Artie Shaw, Hal Borne, and Victor Young, also starring Paulette Goddard, Artie Shaw, Burgess Meredith, and Charles Butterworth.

1941 September 25	*You'll Never Get Rich* is released, with music by Cole Porter, also starring Rita Hayworth.
1942 March 28	Ava Astaire is born.
1942 June 15	*Holiday Inn* is released, directed by Mark Sandrich, with music by Irving Berlin, also starring Bing Crosby and Marjorie Reynolds.
1942 October 5	*You Were Never Lovelier* is released, with music by Jerome Kern, also starring Rita Hayworth.
1943 July 13	*The Sky's the Limit* is released, with music by Johnny Mercer, also starring Joan Leslie, Robert Benchley, and Eric Blore.
1944 March	Lord Charles Cavendish dies in Ireland.
1945 October 19	*Yolanda and the Thief* is released, directed by Vincente Minnelli, with music by Arthur Freed, also starring Lucille Bremer.
1946	Fred Astaire's horse Triplicate wins the Hollywood Park Gold Cup.
1946 January 11	*Ziegfeld Follies* is released, directed by Vincente Minnelli.
1946 September 26	*Blue Skies* is released, with music by Irving Berlin, also starring Bing Crosby.
1947 April 28	Adele Astaire marries Kingman Douglass in Virginia.
1948 June 1	*Easter Parade* is released, directed by Charles Walters, with music by Irving Berlin, also starring Judy Garland, Peter Lawford, and Ann Miller.
1949 March 23	Fred Astaire receives a special award from the Academy of Motion Picture Arts and Sciences.
1949 April 11	*The Barkleys of Broadway* is released, directed by Charles Walters, with music by Ira Gershwin and Arthur Freed, also starring Ginger Rogers and Oscar Levant.
1950 July 12	*Three Little Words* is released, also starring Red Skelton, Vera-Ellen, and Debbie Reynolds.
1950 August 11	*Let's Dance* is released, also starring Betty Hutton.
1951 February 14	*Royal Wedding* is released, directed by Stanley Donen, with music by Arthur Jay Lerner, also starring Jane Powell, Peter Lawford, and Sarah Churchill.
1952 February 28	*The Belle of New York* is released, directed by Charles Walters, with music by Johnny Mercer.

1953 July 7	*The Band Wagon* is released, directed by Vincente Minnelli, with music by Howard Dietz and Arthur Schwartz, also starring Cyd Charisse, Oscar Levant, and Jack Buchanan.
1954 September 13	Phyllis Astaire dies.
1955 May 4	*Daddy Long Legs* is released, with music by Johnny Mercer, also starring Leslie Caron.
1957 February 13	*Funny Face* is released, directed by Stanley Donen, with music by Ira and George Gershwin, Leonard Gershe, and Roger Edens, also starring Audrey Hepburn and Kay Thompson.
1957 May 20	*Silk Stockings* is released, with music by Cole Porter, also starring Cyd Charisse and Peter Lorre.
1958 October 17	"An Evening with Fred Astaire" is shown on NBC, also starring Barrie Chase, and wins nine Emmys.
1959 November 4	"Another Evening with Fred Astaire" is shown on NBC, also starring Barrie Chase.
1959 December 2	*On the Beach*, Fred Astaire's first dramatic film, is released, also starring Gregory Peck, Ava Gardner, and Anthony Perkins.
1960 September 28	"Astaire Time" is shown on NBC, also starring Barrie Chase, and wins two Emmys.
1961 May 8	*The Pleasure of His Company* is released, also starring Debbie Reynolds, Lilli Palmer, and Tab Hunter.
1962 June 26	*The Notorious Landlady* is released, also staring Kim Novak, Jack Lemmon, and Lionel Jeffries.
1964 October 2	"Think Pretty," a musical drama, is shown on NBC, also starring Barrie Chase.
1968 October 9	*Finian's Rainbow* is released, directed by Francis Ford Coppola, also starring Petula Clark and Tommy Steele.
1968 February 7	"The Fred Astaire Show" is shown on NBC, also starring Barrie Chase.
1969 May 15	*The Midas Run* is released, also starring Anne Heywood, Richard Crenna, Roddy McDowall, and Ralph Richardson.
1972 January 17	" 'S Wonderful, 'S Marvelous, 'S Gershwin" is shown on NBC.
1973	Kingman Douglass, Adele Astaire's second husband, dies.

1974 June 15	*That's Entertainment* is released, directed by Jack Haley, Jr.
1974 December 15	*The Towering Inferno* is released, also starring Steve McQueen, Paul Newman, William Holden, Faye Dunaway, Richard Chamberlain, Jennifer Jones, Robert Wagner, and Robert Vaughn. Fred is nominated for an Oscar for best supporting actor.
1975 July	Ann Astaire dies.
1976	*The Amazing Dobermans* is released.
1976 May 17	*That's Entertainment Part 2* is released, directed by Gene Kelly.
1977	*The Purple Taxi* is released, also starring Charlotte Rampling, Philippe Noiret, and Peter Ustinov.
1980 June 24	Fred Astaire marries Robyn Smith in Hollywood.
1981 January 25	Adele Astaire dies.
1981 April 10	Fred Astaire accepts the Life Achievement Award of the American Film Institute, at the International Ballroom of the Beverly Hilton Hotel.
1981 December 15	*Ghost Story* is released, directed by John Irvin, also starring Douglas Fairbanks, Jr.
1987 June 22	Fred Astaire dies.